Maximilian Schele de Vere

The Romance of American History

Early Annals

Maximilian Schele de Vere

The Romance of American History
Early Annals

ISBN/EAN: 9783337066369

Printed in Europe, USA, Canada, Australia, Japan

Cover: Foto ©ninafisch / pixelio.de

More available books at **www.hansebooks.com**

THE ROMANCE OF AMERICAN HISTORY.

EARLY ANNALS.

BY

M. SCHELE DE VERE.

NEW YORK:
G. P. PUTNAM & SONS,
4TH AVE. & 23D ST.

LONDON: SAMPSON, LOW & CO.
1872.

Entered according to Act of Congress, in the year 1872, by
PUTNAM & SONS,
in the Office of the Librarian of Congress, at Washington.

CONTENTS.

I.
LO THE POOR INDIAN! 1

II.
THE HIDDEN RIVER 33

III.
OUR FIRST ROMANCE 69

IV.
A FEW TOWN-NAMES 101

V.
KAISERS, KINGS AND KNIGHTS 145

VI.
LOST TOWNS 187

VII.
LOST LANDS. 216

ROMANCE

OF

AMERICAN HISTORY.

———◆———

LO! THE POOR INDIAN.

I.

PIOUS COTTON MATHER, with his heart full of sweetness and his wig full of learning, once expressed his opinion of the natives of our land in these remarkable words : " The natives of the country, now possessed by the New Englanders, had been forlorn and wretched heathen ever since their first herding there, and though we know not how and when these Indians first became inhabited of this mighty continent, yet we may guess that probably the *Devil* decoyed these miserable salvages hither, in hopes that the gospel of the Lord Jesus Christ would never reach here, or disturb his absolute empire over them. But our Eliot was on such ill terms with the Devil as to alarm him with sounding the silver trumpets of heaven in his territory, and was willing to rescue as many of them as he could from the old usurping *Landlord* of America, who is, by the wrath of God, the prince of this world." The great divine was, no doubt, sincerely anxious to blow the same trumpet with all the zeal and energy with which he was naturally endowed, but he neglects to explain to us the plea on which his children, the New Englanders, carried on their traffic with this ill-reputed Landlord, and hesitated not to deal with much shrewdness and to good purpose with these children of the Devil. It has been suggested that they thought it but right to ruin and to destroy the tenants of the Evil One, so as to gain room for a better generation, and they themselves more than once quote the example of the Jews spoiling the Egyptians, as a precedent for their own policy.

This charitable view of the parentage of the poor Indian, and of his relations to Satan, were however at one time entertained very generally by learned divines. Thus we find the first biblical scholar of his age, Dr. Joseph Meade, writing in 1634 these words: "The *Devil*, being impatient of the sound of the Gospel and the Cross of Christ in every part of this old world, so that he could in no place be quiet for it, and foreseeing that he was like at length to lose all here, bethought himself to provide him of a seed, over which he might reign securely. He accordingly drew a colony out of some of those barbarous nations, dwelling upon the ocean, whether the sound of the Gospel had not yet come, and promising then by some oracle to show them a country far better than their own, pleasant and large, where man never yet inhabited, he conducted them over those desert lands and isles by the way of the North into America. And there did the Devil ever reign more absolutely and without control since mankind first fell under his clutches." It is hard to imagine why the poor race of red men, already so unmistakably doomed to destruction, should have been denounced, in addition, as the offspring of Satan and his own peculiar people. The sons of the pilgrims evidently needed no such argument to enforce their policy: when the Indian resisted, they had a right to smite him hip and thigh ; when disease destroyed him and his children in their sight, the Lord showed them by His dispensation that the land was cleared for their benefit, and if a good bargain in land could be had they were ready to pay a fair price in boots, bumbo, and Bibles.

There is some comfort, therefore, in a kindly suggestion made by Dr. Twiss, afterwards Prolocutor of the Westminster Assembly, when replying to Dr. Meade's above mentioned letter: " Considering our English plantations of late, and the opinions of many grave divines concerning the Gospel's fleeting westwards sometimes, I have had such thoughts: why may not this be the place of New Jerusalem?" He does not deny the Satanic descent of the poor Indians ; on the contrary, to him also they are sons of Belial and "children of perdition," but at least he does not speak of the Devil as our Landlord and absolute ruler. We may reasonably hope, therefore, that the whole doctrine of Satanic origin rested only upon a desire to increase the zeal for their conversion and to deepen the sympathy for their unhappy condition.

The warm heart of brave Captain Smith, ever overflowing with kindly feeling for the poor salvages, and leading him, out of his scanty means, to set aside £200 for their conversion, saw in them, not the children of the Devil, not at least an accursed race. When in the month of April, 1614, with two ships from London he (I) "chanced to arrive in New England, a part of Ameryca," he fell in with the Indians there, and whether they struck him as different from the Powhatans of his beloved Virginia, or merely recalled to him early impressions, he stated that "some conceive the inhabitants of New England to be Ham's posterity, and consequently shut out from grace by Noah's curse till the conversion of the Jews be past at least."

It is certainly not a little curious that this idea of a Jewish origin of our native neighbors should have so often recurred to the minds of early discoverers, even where no previous impression of the kind could have prepared them for such a notion. William Penn, it is well-known, adopted the view that they were of Jewish origin ; and at the South, the same opinion has been entertained by men well acquainted, through personal intercourse, with all their peculiarities.

Thus James Adair, an Englishman of learning and great enterprise, who lived for more than thirty years among the Chickasaws, and had frequent intercourse with the Cherokees, Choctaw, and Muscogees, published in 1775 a work on American Indians, in which he proved himself well acquainted with Hebrew, and, as was to be expected, a perfect master of various Indian idioms. He was firmly convinced that the red men of the South, at least, were the descendants of one of the lost tribes of Israel, who had preserved, with the exception of circumcision, all the leading features of old testamentary worship. He had found among them the name of Jehovah but slightly altered, and attributed to the one supreme God; he had recognized in their religious chants a distinct hallelujah, and had seen, with his own eyes, a grand temple of theirs, to which the tribes came up in their order, where priests presented burnt offerings and thanks offerings, and even a Holy of Holies. His convictions were reiterated by a man who seemed to be still better qualified to judge of the curious question,—Abram Mordecai, himself a Jew, and a man of equal intelligence and learning, who spent fifty years of his life among the Creeks, and, as late as the year 1847, expressed his firm belief that the latter were members of the same race to which he also belonged.

A very clever German, Gerard de Brahm, who was long "Surveyor for the Southern District of America," much addicted to alchemy, but remarkably shrewd in all other matters of worldly interest, also spent a large portion of his life, from 1756 to 1771, among these Southern Indians, and, strangely enough, came to the same conclusion. He went even farther than the English authors in tracing their descent, for he claimed for his special friends, the Cherokees, an unbroken pedigree from no less a personage than Noah's son, Japhet. He maintained that the silence observed in Holy Writ as to all the sons of Japhet, with the exception of the oldest, proved their having, at an early period of history, absented themselves from the rest of Noah's generations. The fact that the Pentateuch makes no mention at all of what became of Magog and his four brothers, and only speaks of them as hunters, pursuing their father's favorite passion, appears to him sufficient proof that they must have strayed away to remote parts of the earth, from whence neither history nor tradition could reach those who remained in Assyria. These wandering hunters, sons of the man who was told that he should "dwell in tents," and brothers of him who "dissolves," were in all probability cut off from the European continent in the time of Peleg, the son of Noah's grandson, when the world, according to sacred history, was "separated." Why he should have counted in only his special friends and neighbors among the children of Magog, the eccentric German does not tell us; but without hesitation he adds that the Southern Indians are evidently descendants of the ancient Carthaginians, who, in their days, as the great merchants of the universe, discovered by their trading vessels many islands and sent colonies to improve them. Probably some of these vessels, in pursuit of their discovery, recognizing the more Southern shore, fell in with the trade-winds, and, not experienced in sailing upon the wind, were blown into the Gulf of Mexico, while the Carthaginian navigators carried with them the knowledge of conveying their history to posterity by hieroglyphics, from which the Northern Indians have learned to leave their particular adventures and martial exploits with red and black on trees nearest by as evidences of the truth."

Nor is this idea of a Jewish origin confined to the earlier days of our history. Richard Peters, a gentleman of superior intelligence and high character, who, for various reasons, had been intimately acquainted with several tribes of Indians, and become especially so endeared to the Tuscaroras as to be adopted by them under the name of Tegochtias, the Paroquet, entertained the same views, based upon careful inquiry and personal knowledge. "If they are of Israelitish descent, it is in the decrees of Providence," he says, "that, like all other Jews, they must be homeless wanderers, dispersed throughout all the regions of the earth. Even now, in our day (1825), a portion of these copper-colored Ishmaelites, if so they be, are to be compelled to wander far away and leave their cultivated fields." The argument sounds as if taken from one of those fanatic sermons by which, in the early middle ages, zealous priests endeavored to arouse their hearers to a crusade against the poor Jews of Germany. The effect is, certainly, if not so immediate, quite as unfailing.

After having thus been denounced as the children of Satan, and homeless descendants of an accursed race, the poor red men of our continent can, with stoic indifference, bear all other genealogies, which have been provided for them by learned and unlearned men. What can it matter to them, whether they are endowed by self-constituted Herald's Colleges with ancestors from Iceland or from Japan? They might easily retort that, as this continent, the New World, is beyond all doubt the Old World by eminence, and dates back from times long anterior to the annals of Europe at least, so their race also may perhaps have a pedigree far older than the Rohans of France, who accompanied Noah into his ark. Or they can, if so inclined, accept Agassiz's theory, which gives them a first father of their own, an Adam who deserves his name of the red one far more truly than the familiar first man of our schools.

On the other hand, we find missionaries especially inclined to attribute their want of success among the Indians to some occult element in their character. For it is a remarkable fact that the efforts of the most pious and most zealous men at the North and in the South have remained equally sterile. We need only recall such truly great men as the Apostle of the Indians, his brethren of New England, and the noble host of martyrs among the Moravians, from a Mayhew and a Loskiel down to our own day. "Loskiel could not change the Indian character," says Bancroft, curtly but sadly. All traces of Eliot's labors disappeared with himself. "Not one Indian Christian was gathered by the English missionaries in Connecticut," says Trumbull in his history of that

State. One of the most striking instances of such a failure of permanent conversion was the island known as Martha's Vineyard. Discovered in May, 1602, its inhabitants had, in less than fifty years, "embraced Christianity and adopted English manners and customs in husbandry and other concerns," thanks to the indefatigable labors of the noble Mayhews.

In 1660 there were about three thousand Christian Indians on the island, with ministers of their own race—and a generation later, the whole had vanished like a dream! Nor was it otherwise among other tribes. The pathetic stories of Praying Indians, the terrible massacres of Cherry Valley and of Wyoming, and the martyrdom of converts in Moravian settlements, all speak loudly in behalf of the efforts made to convert the red man—all point as clearly to the inefficiency of these attempts. Virginia in vain opened her schools and colleges to her Indians; Penn the Quaker, and Oglethorpe the Philanthropist, tried in vain to win them over by kindness and unremitting solicitations. There are, no doubt, communities, and perhaps even tribes like the Christian Cherokees, who have adopted Christianity as they have accepted the benefits of civilization; but the race as such was never converted, though living in a Christian land, and by the side of such grateful examples we have pointed out to us other tribes dwelling in our midst and still offering sacrifices to their idols and practising all the abominations of their forefathers.

It cannot be denied that as long as the Indian is a

nomad, so long will he also remain a heathen. And will he ever cease to be a wanderer over the surface of the earth? In a question so closely affecting the most powerful interests of a great nation, it is very difficult to ascertain the truth. Indian commissioners, unbiassed travellers, pious missionaries, all differ in the most startling manner, when their opinion on this subject is asked. To the one, nothing appears simpler than to tame the Indian; to the other, he is a genuine wild asses colt.

One feature, however, in the Indian's character is too well proven to be questioned. This is the irresistible charm which the wild life of the plains and the woods has ever had for those even among them who have had the sweets of civilization, and have fully acquired the habits of refined society. Examples are not wanting, from the earliest days of our colonial life to comparatively recent days. When Virginia was still in her infancy she established a college "for educating infidel children in the knowledge of the true God," and added to it, at a little distance from Henrico, an East India school for Indians especially. Her efforts were blasted by the terrible massacre of 1622, when all the white settlers of the colony, save a handful, were butchered in cold blood. But undismayed, she went to work once more, and soon a University of Henrico was laid off, which was "intended as well for a college for the education of Indians, as also to lay the foundation of a seminary of learning for the English" (Stith. Virginia, p. 163). A third attempt was made when the College of William and Mary was established at Williamsburg, but with what success? We have the report of a contemporary : "And here I must lament the bad success Mr. Boyle's charity has hitherto had towards converting any of those poor heathens to Christianity. Many children of our Indian neighbors have been brought up in the College of William and Mary. They have been taught to read and write, and been carefully instructed in the principles of the Christian religion, till they came to the age of manhood. Yet, after they returned home, instead of converting and civilizing the rest, they have immediately relapsed into barbarism and infidelity themselves." And this is the invariable result. At a later period Governor Spotswood also sent a certain number of children, the sons of the great men of several Indian tribes, who had been taken as hostages during the war in South Carolina, to William and Mary College. They were taught, they were converted, and when they returned to their homes they resumed the blanket, and with it all the habits of their heathen brethren! In another part of Virginia, a Mr. Charles Griffin, a man of good family, of immaculate character and great sweetness of temper, was placed as schoolmaster among the Sappon's Indians, and devoted himself for years with matchless zeal and judicious energy to the task of educating them and preparing them for civilized life. All the pains he took had but the effect " to make them somewhat cleanlier than the other Indians," as we are told in Col. William Byrd's interesting Journal. The latter naively adds that the only way to civilize and Christianize Indians is to intermarry with them, concluding with this quaint remark: "It is strange that any good Christian should have refused a wholesome, straight bedfellow, when he might have so fair a portion with her as the merit of saving her soul." Still another school at Christina, on the Nottoway River, where, at one time, seventy Indian children were daily taught in a handsome school-house, specially built for their benefit, ended in the same disastrous manner. They could train the Indian's mind, but they seemed to be unable to change his heart.

Nor were individual efforts more successful. As early as the year 1659, an English merchant, John Beauchamp, obtained permission from the General Assembly of Virginia, to carry his Indian boy "into England, provided that, at the County Court in Charles City County, he make it appear that he hath the consent of the said Indian boy's parents soe to doe" (Heming's Reports I. p. 546). He obtained the required consent, he took the boy to his house in England and gave him an excellent education. Young Beauchamp, as he was called after his benefactor, returned a grown man to the colony, went to visit his brethren on the upper waters of the Dan— and never returned, sending only yearly messages of kindness and good-will to his friends among the English.

General Oglethorpe also took, in 1743, an Indian boy, the son of one of the greatest chiefs in Georgia, with him to England, animated by an earnest desire to make him, at any expense and by every effort on his part, a fit instrument to carry the advantages of civilization and the blessings of Christianity to his unfortunate brethren. The youth received a liberal education, the best that England could afford in those days, and became a polished man, moving freely in the best society and perfectly at home in all the details even of courtly life. He then went back to his tribe, the Creeks, and great were the expectations of his noble old friend, and high the hopes of all who wished well to the Indians, when he parted with them at Savannah. A fine portrait of General Oglethorpe, with his young Indian friend standing in an affectionate attitude by his side, commemorated the event, and was long kept in the Garden City of the South, till the British captured the town in 1778, and destroyed the picture. But the result was the same sad disappointment. In a short time the accomplished courtier became a wily Indian once more; he laid aside his European costume, and with it the habits he had acquired in England, and before a short year had passed he had become an Indian warrior once more in the full and most painful sense of the word.

The French also tried the experiment more than once. Their first effort already, though not without its whimsical features, ended in the most disastrous manner. A young, gallant Frenchman had been sent up to the mouth of the Missouri to purchase land there and to erect a fort, which he was to hold with a small garrison. He found himself surrounded there by Indians on all sides, and to while away his time during an interval of peace, he filled their minds with glowing pictures of French life, and excited their imagination to the utmost by vivid accounts of the splendor of his sovereign's court. When they were wrought up to the highest point he took advantage of the excitement to bribe, by means of promises and presents, eleven principal men, together with the fair daughter of the chief of a tribe, to accompany him to France. They sailed merrily down the great river; they rested a few weeks at New Orleans, where the beautiful princess with her strange retinue created much excitement, and then embarked for Europe. Such a novelty as an Indian princess, accompanied by eleven full-plumed savages in all their war-paint, was a most welcome event to the weary Parisians, and the novel embassy was received with much pomp, and actually invited to appear at court. Even the honor of being presented to the king's majesty, however, does not seem to have exempted the poor Indians from the necessity of catering to the curiosity of the Parisians; they were made to hunt deer in the Bois de Boulogne after their own fashion of the western prairies, and at the Italian Theatre to exhibit their national dances. In the meantime the priests had been busy with the royal lady, and great was the delight of the populace when on a fine summer day a double ceremony was announced to take place in the great Cathedral of Notre Dame. The Indian princess, as she was always styled, was solemnly received into the bosom of the Christian Church in the morning, and in the afternoon married to a Sergeant Dubois, who had accompanied the strange travellers, and was now, as a reward for his success, made an officer and appointed " Commander of the Missouris." The excitement was intense. Church and State alike looked forward to the great advantages that were to be derived from such an alliance of the daughter of a great Indian chieftain with a Frenchman, and their united influence over a great and powerful nation. All the court-ladies brought rich presents for the happy couple, and the King himself deigned to add new favors. The eleven warriors appeared in new blue coats covered with gold lace, and hats adorned with plumes and gorgeous cockades, while the lucky author of the enterprise was made a knight of St. Louis, married a rich widow, and quietly remained in France thereafter. Mr. and Mrs. Dubois, with their suite, were then sent back in great state on board a national vessel, and when they reached New Orleans well-cared for and hospitably entertained by the agents of Law's famous though ill-fated Mississippi company, with a view to future trading advantages on the upper river. The company also furnished them with a ship to reach their distant homes; an armed guard was detailed to accompany them, and amid loud shouts and enthusiastic cheers they left the city. But still greater was the joy and still louder the enthusiasm when, after a long and tedious voyage, they reached at last the home of their brethren, the Missouris. There was no end of rejoicing and feasting to celebrate the return of the chieftain's daughter and the eleven doughty warriors, and when the vessel turned once more southward every heart was full of hope and every mind busy with the vast profit that France was to reap from this cunning measure. Alas! the ship was barely out of sight when the princess reappeared in all the touching simplicity of her national costume, and that very night her husband and the whole little garrison were cruelly butchered! "Thus, this post no longer exists," adds plaintively the chronicles of the tragic event.—(Dumont Mem. Hist. sur la Louisiane II. p. 78.)

A similar effort made at a much later period by no less a personage than General Lafayette, ended less tragically, but in a manner equally disheartening. He had taken an infant son of Corn Planter, chief of one of the so-called Six Nations, to France with him, principally for the purpose of testing the capacity of his race for moral improvement. The best masters were provided, the highest society opened its doors, and no effort was spared to make the young chieftain an accomplished man of the world. When he reached manhood there seemed to be nothing more wanting to his education; he satisfied the most fastidious taste in his manners and his principles, and finally he even won the affections of a beautiful woman, who married him with the consent of her friends and relations. With her he returned to this country. "He was about twenty-six years of age, of an active genius, and very friendly to the United States," says a newspaper of that day,—the American Apollo of Boston. On the morning of his arrival he was visited by many prominent men who had been interested in the young man and his mission; they found him all they had been led to expect— a gay but elegant Frenchman, with all the marks of good breeding in speech and in manners. When he returned at night to his hotel the powder and the silk stockings had vanished, he was half drunk, and nearly unconscious of what he had been doing. The next day, however, he declared his intention to accompany some Indians, whom he had met in the streets, to their home; they happened to be men of his own tribe, Oneidas, and had been on a visit to the Government of the United States. When next seen he was surrounded by them, brutally drunk and wrapped in a blanket; he returned with his newly-found brethren, leaving his loving wife on the way, cruelly abused and stripped of her property. Thus she was found by Aaron Burr as he was travelling from Canada to New York; almost naked and subsisting on berries and wild fruit. The young chieftain disappeared in his native forests for nearly three years; then he was suddenly seen once more in the streets of Philadelphia, a miserable wreck, debauched and disfigured almost beyond recognition, and before help could be extended to him, he died there in 1792.—(The American Apollo, Boston 1792.)

Startling as these well authenticated examples of red men are, who could not be weaned from their true nature by all the wiles and blandishments of civilization, there is greater wonder still in the apparently irresistible charm which Indian life has had for white men, who have once fallen under the influence of its strange attractions. The hope of Governor Spotswood, that intermarriage between the two races might at last succeed in civilizing the natives, was unconsciously refuted by an able and careful observer, the Marquis of Denonville, who, in 1685, wrote to the French Government: "It has long been believed that it is necessary to mingle with the Indians in order to Frenchify (franciser) them. But this is a mistake. Those with whom we mingle do not become French, but our people become Indians!" No one, who has ever seen the Canadian voyageurs on Northern waters, or the now nearly extinct French half-breeds in the far west, can doubt the correctness of this assertion. This fondness for Indian life is, however, by no means limited to the lower classes. No reader of our early annals will ever forget the strange story of Colonel Castine, a Frenchman of noble birth, of large fortune and brilliant antecedents. For some time commanding the regiment of Carignan, his wit and his abilities were such as to attract, long afterwards, the admiration of Raynal and of Voltaire, both of whom speak of him in terms of admiration. All of a sudden, and for reasons which have never become known, he determined to leave France and to seek a new home in America. Purchasing some land on the Penobscot River, he settled down there, married the daughter of a chief, and spent the remainder of his life with the Indians. His eldest son, "an influential sachem with a number of wives, which he had selected from the natives" (Sullivan, Maine, p. 258), became the bitter enemy of the English. It so happened that a new frontier line being drawn in consequence of the Treaty of Breda, Castine's seat fell into the patent granted to James

II. as Duke of York, and this gave a pretext—it is hard to tell how—to the commander of an English frigate to plunder Castine's house from roof to cellar. The young hot-headed half-breed, animated by the double insult done to the French nobleman and the Indian Sagamore, for he was then chief sachem of the Penobscots, resented the brutal injury deeply, and made the English pay dearly for the rash measure during many a war to which he incited the tribes under his control.

Nor was it by any means Gallic levity alone which thus readily fraternized with the red Indian and adopted his habits. Even the steady German, most cosmopolitan of all nations at home, and the last to lay aside his nationality abroad, could not resist the strange charm. He was, on the contrary, among the very first who appear in the annals of our history as having cast in their lot with the savages and joined them in times of peace or on the warpath. Blunt Captain John Smith does not hesitate to speak of some Germans whom he had courteously sent to King Powhatan to build him a house after European fashion, as "those damned Dutchmen." (Purchas. IV., 1721.) At first sight they appear to deserve the harsh name. For after reaching the "Empereur's" house they turned from their English friends, joined the Indians, and refused to return or to aid those by whom they had been sent. But upon a more careful examination a valid excuse is found for their apparent treachery. John Smith tells us with a strange unconsciousness of the nature of his proposal that he had used the building of a house for

Powhatan as a pretext, his real aim being to use the Germans as spies and auxiliaries in his cunning scheme to seize upon the person of the king and to hold him as hostage in Jamestown! The poor "Dutchmen," as they were called after the manner of those days, were either too honest or too timid to carry out the project; they revealed or confessed the plan, and when John Smith escaped with the aid of Pocahontas, the Germans were forgiven on condition that they should be adopted into some Indian families and make their wigwam their home for the future. They disappear in the darkness of Indian history; but the charm was as potent thereafter as ever before. For only a few years later a Swiss, called Volday, being sent to bring them home, became himself so enchanted with Indian life that he also remained. Only one of the Germans, Adams, returned to Jamestown, where he received his pardon, although he was probably the one whom "the President had placed as a spy upon Powhatan, being a man of judgment and resolution, and therefore thought most proper." (Stith. Va., p. 86.) A couple of others paid dearly for lusting after the fleshpots of the red men. "In time of trouble" they went to Powhatan and promised, that if well received, they would do wonders for him upon the arrival of Lord Delaware. But the cunning savage said that men so ready to betray John Smith would be equally ready to betray him, if they could gain anything, and "had their brains beaten out."

It was more than two generations later when another German appears in our annals with the war-paint on his body and the tomahawk in his hand. Though miscalled by French writers, who speak of him as Hiens, he bore the characteristic name of his nation, Hans, and is called "a flibustier whom M. de la Salle had taken to go with him on this expedition." (Iontel, rédigé par M. de Michel, Paris, 1713, p. 208). He was present when his master, the great and rich Governor of the Haramuch, was murdered in cold blood by a couple of miscreants, one of whom, Listot, a surgeon by profession, cried to him as he dispatched him : " There you are, grand Bashaw, there you are ! " He was shocked and grieved, but helpless, and not brave enough to interfere, and when the conspirators struck inland, leaving La Salle unburied on the wild coast of Texas, and the place of his death unmarked even by an humble cross, he timidly followed his brutal companions as they set out on their famous journey from the Gulf of Mexico to the waters of the St. Lawrence. He soon disappeared, however, from the pages of their remarkable journal. The last that is seen of him is the vast outline of his bulky person on horseback rising dim and dark against a lowering Western sky, as he accompanied his new friends, the Cenis Indians, on the warpath against hostile tribes. Unwilling, as he told Jouttel, to return to France merely to have his head taken off by a man in a mask, and fortified by a written certificate in Latin, that he had taken no share in La Salle's murder, he had quietly settled down among the Indians, assumed their garb, married a squaw, and secured their respect and admiration. Thus exit Hans in 1687.

Probably the two most remarkable instances of warm attachment to Indian life recorded in our history are those of a Jesuit and of a New England minister's daughter, the one in the far South of the present Union, the other in the home of the Puritans.

In the year 1736 there appeared among the Cherokees and their allies one of the most extraordinary persons that has ever threatened the peace and security of our land. This was a small, wiry man, whose open countenance looked all candor and kindness, while his eyes fairly shone with intelligence and seemed to have the power to search the hearts of man to their innermost recesses. No one could have guessed at his nationality, for he had in all respects adopted the Indian costumes and observed their peculiarities down to the minutest detail. Painted in the strange manner of a medicine man, covered from head to foot with dangling teeth and tails and toes of every brute and beast of the forest, he ate and drank and danced like the most fanatic of Indian conjurors. At the same time he discreetly used his superior knowledge so as not to shock his Indian brethren by any assumption of pride, and yet rendering himself eminently useful to them in times of war and of peace. No wonder, therefore, that he soon obtained an almost absolute sway over the minds of the Cherokees and other neighboring tribes, and availed himself of this strangely won power to indulge in his deadly hatred of the English. His influence grew stronger from day to day; his insulting messages sent to the colonial authorities became more and more intolerable, and at last South Carolina dispatched a Colonel Fox to arrest this dangerous person. The English officer was courteously received as a "beloved man," and solemnly led to the great square before the Council House of the tribe ; there he saw, to his dismay, the mysterious person whom he had come to arrest, treated on all sides with unbounded respect and surrounded by a powerful body-guard. He was allowed to make known his errand ; the farce of a solemn council to deliberate on the message was performed, and then the "beloved man" was advised to withdraw instantly, while the formidable stranger, with cutting irony, placed some of his guards at his disposal. It seems, however, that gradually he became over-secure in his self-conceit, and thus, in the year 1744, he started on his way to Mobile, accompanied only by a few Cherokee warriors and unarmed. He was recognized by some settlers on his path, captured by them, and carried to the Fort of Frederica, where General Oglethorpe was then residing.

When he was brought up for examination, the British officers found, to their utmost amazement, under the hideous paint and the coarse and fantastic dress of deerskin and Indian mocassins, a man of the most polished address and the highest abilities. He spoke Latin and French, English and Spanish to perfection, and seemed to be equally familiar with all the dialects of Southern Indian tribes. Nor did he for a moment hesitate to make known his history or to avow his purposes. He was a German, Christian Preber, a member of the Society of

Jesus, and had been sent by his superior to the Indians of South Carolina. Here he had speedily conceived the plan of forming at Cupeta, a part of Georgia still held by the Cherokees, a grand rallying place for discontented Europeans, fugitives from English justice, deserters from French garrisons, and starving Germans escaping from unsuccessful settlements, and runaway negroes. To all of these he offered here an asylum and the means of livelihood till they could be employed in his great enterprise. This was nothing less than to form a vast confederation of all the Southern Indians, to inspire them with the love of industry, to instruct them in the arts and handicraft of civilized life, and thus, at the proper time, to enable them to throw off the yoke of European colonists, and to repossess themselves of their native soil! And to this purpose he had devoted, not only his life, but the whole vigor of his energetic intellect, the vast scope of his knowledge and the marvellous power he possessed in swaying the minds of men. In his MSS. was found a complete and admirable scheme of government for the future Indian confederacy, in which nothing was forgotten and every department was elaborated down to the minutest detail, and so firm was his belief in the ultimate success of his plans that he coolly said to the court-martial before which he was summoned: "Believe me, before the century is passed, the Europeans will have a very small footing on this continent!"

This self-reliance was not to be shaken by such a slight mishap as his captivity. He bore his confinement and all the attendant privations with imperturbable equanimity. His quarters were near the arsenal; a fire broke out there, and amid a fearful explosion of shells and many tons of powder, the whole group of buildings was wrapped in sheets of flame. Everybody expected to find the prisoner dead, but to the boundless surprise of those who first ventured near the scene of the terrible disaster, he was discovered in his log cabin, which had escaped as by a miracle, calmly reading a favorite Greek author. When they asked him why he had made no effort to escape, he coolly told them, that exploding shells were dangerous neighbors, and the safest place, in his opinion, was close by them, as few, if any, would fall back precisely to the place from whence they came, and thus he had quietly remained where he was, and escaped unharmed. It is difficult to imagine how formidable a man of such marvellous endowments might have become to the infant colonies of the South; but, fortunately for their peace, he died suddenly while yet a captive, and before his Indian brethren could come to his rescue.

Very different, and yet by no means less strange, was the wayward fancy which changed a pious minister's tender child into an Indian squaw, and made her prefer the wild life of the woods to her place by the hearth of her home. During a fierce stormy winter night of the year 1704, three hundred French and Indian soldiers, under Hertel de Ronville, fell upon the peaceful village of Deerfield in Massachusetts, plundering, burning, and slaying. They seized the pastor of the little flock, the

Rev. John Williams, and carried him, his wife, and six of his children as captives to Canada. On the second day his beloved wife succumbed ; she sank exhausted by the side of the narrow path and was instantly tomahawked ; twenty prisoners shared her terrible fate, before they reached their destination in Canada,—for the sufferings were terrible, the pace furious, and the weather severe, even for a Canadian winter. There were no provisions dealt out, save a handful of ground nuts at times, or a few acorns; now and then a bunch of purslain or bogweed was thrown into the kettle, and twice or thrice, on the journey, a small supply of dog's-flesh was doled out to the poor captives. They had no clothes, for they had been completely stripped when taken from their houses, no shoes, no stockings—nothing but a thin blanket for each prisoner to cover his nakedness, and a few leather stockings distributed among them to keep their feet from perishing with cold. In this plight they were forced to travel twenty and thirty miles a day, carrying heavy burdens for their masters, and threatened with instant death if they lagged but for a moment. Oh, who can fathom the grief of a father's heart as he saw the wife of his bosom slain in cold blood, and the children of his old age sink, one by one, in mortal agony, by the wayside !

Fortunately the captives, when they reached Canada, fell into the hands of the French, and were, by them, treated with humanity, and even with kindness. Two years later, the Rev. Mr. Williams and two of his children were redeemed in Boston ; the unhappy father returned like a faithful shepherd to his little flock at Deerfield, and became known all over the colonies as The Redeemed Captive, partly from his terrible story, and partly from an account of his sufferings and trials, which he published under that title. But the strangest part of the adventure remains to be told. His youngest daughter, Eunice, who was but seven years old when the fatal event occurred, had been adopted into a family of Praying Indians near Montreal, and refused to accompany her father and her brothers when they returned to the colonies. With a heavy heart they left her in the hands of their enemies, and trusted that with advancing years an awakening sense of her natural relations to her race and her family would change her views. But it was far otherwise. She married one of the chiefs of the tribe among whom she lived, called Cahnewaga, and all solicitations from family, friends, and visitors to return to her house and to abandon her Catholic faith proved unavailing. Even when she was at last persuaded to visit her relatives in New England, when the whole village turned out to receive their beloved pastor's long-lost daughter, and proved the sincerity of their deep sympathy by keeping a day of fast, and by assembling to pray in concert for her delivery, she remained firm in her attachment to Indian life. She persisted in wearing the blanket and counting her beads, and although urged and besought by her two brothers, both worthy ministers of the gospel, to remain with them, she returned, after each visit, unchanged to the fires of her wigwam and the love of her own Mohawk children. (Bancroft III. p. 214.)

With such striking examples before our eyes we need not wonder if the stern old Puritans, in their instinctive dread of all witchery and weird spells, attributed a satanic descent to the poor Indians. Here were men and women alike, bred amid all the benign influences of civilization, and early taught the great doctrines of our faith, unable to resist the magic charm of Indian life, whether they entered upon it as tender children, tasted its sweets as young men in the full vigor of early manhood, or resorted to it in declining years, and weary of the vanity and vexation of spirit inherent in the artificial society of older countries. It avails little to be told by a Mather, or even an Edwards, that the woods were full of the Devil's lures, and the very beasts of the fields possessed by evil spirits, which tempted men to join them in savage life and to worship abominable idols. Nor can we imagine a pious minister's child to have been attracted by the cunning arts and wicked tricks which Indian women employed to enhance their beauty and to increase their attractions. For the Rev. Mr. Johnson, of Woburn, Mass., records in his "Wonder-Working Providence" with horror and detestation the shocking discovery he had made, that "their squaws use the sinful art of painting their faces." The charm is not to be sought for on the surface, and the mystery must needs remain unsolved, till some Tannhäuser shall return from the Venus Mountain of Indian hunting grounds and frankly tell us the spell that bewitched his eye and beguiled his heart.

It is not altogether improbable that with an instinctive view to counteract such diabolical spells of Indian magic, an effort was made, at an early day in our history, to canonize one of their most famous chieftains. It seems that there is not far from Doylestown in Pennsylvania a beautiful, endless spring, which gushes full and crystal clear from the mountain-side, and then flows merrily off, a good-sized brook, to fall at some little distance into the Neshaminy River. By the side of this spring, under the shade of a few noble sycamores, a green mound is pointed out as the last resting-place upon earth of Saint Tammany. A native of this locality, Tamané, as William Penn wrote his name, or Tamanend, as he was called by others, he remained there till he came of age, but then crossed with his tribe, the Alleghanies, and went down to the rich hunting-fields of what is now the State of Ohio. By his bravery and his wisdom he rose, towards the middle of the seventeenth century, to become one of the leading sachems among the Lenni-Lenapé, and to make his name familiar to the ear of all settlers in the colonies. For he was from the beginning a warm and staunch friend of the whites, and to him they owed the peace that for a time reigned along the border and enabled them to secure new homes for thousands of their suffering brethren. When old age crept over him, and he was no longer able to lead in war, he resigned his high dignity, appointed an able successor, and retired to his early home in Berks County. Here he was constantly visited by Indians of all tribes and nations, and by whites from the adjoining colonies. Whenever he was called upon to settle disputes or to decide grave questions, he had but one wise counsel to give : Unity—in peace for happiness, in war for defence! Thus the old chieftain grew in renown, and his fame spread far and near ; when, at last, he was gathered to his fathers, his name survived him for generations, and red men and whites alike revered the wise, peace-loving sachem. The name was preserved among the Indians as a noble title of honor, and conferred, from time to time, upon those who seemed to deserve such high distinction. A certain Colonel George Morgan, for instance, who had been sent from Princeton to some of the Western tribes, by order of Congress, endeared himself so much to them by his great gentleness and goodness, that the Delawares bestowed upon him, in 1776, in solemn council, the name of their venerated chief. Morgan brought back with him such a wonderful account of Tamané, that the Continental troops during the war, casting about for a rallying cry to oppose the hated St. George of the British, dubbed the great Indian a saint, and hailed him as St. Tamanend. As such he soon appeared in some almanacs, as we are assured by Hechewelder, and not long after the name was inscribed on the flags of the Pennsylvania troops under Washington's command.

He had, however, in other states, even before that date, received the honor of canonization, and some day in early May, varying from the first to the twelfth, was generally chosen as the Indian Saints' Day. Tammany societies were organized everywhere, processions held, and mysteries solemnized. Thus we read already in

1774 : " Yesterday was celebrated in this place (Norfolk, Va.,) the anniversary of St. Tammany, the tutelar Saint of the American colonies. After the ladies had retired, towards 4 o'clock A.M., the Sons of Tammany, according to the immemorial custom of these countries, encircled their king and practised the ancient, mysterious war-dance, so highly descriptive of the warmest attachment and freedom of spirit." (Va. Gazette, May 3, 1774.) Nor was the saint's popularity less great farther South. A small village on Roanoke River, in Mecklenburg County, Va., bears still the name of St. Tammany, and so does a parish in Louisiana, lying between the Mississippi and Lake Pontchartrain.

How the poor saint subsequently was drummed out of the army, by special order of the Secretary of War, because his festival "tended to debauchery among the troops," how he was welcomed by the Democrats of New York, and installed with great pomp and circumstance as the patron saint of a powerful branch of that party, and how he finally ruled supreme in the Empire State, and well-nigh threatened to exact abject worship from a whole nation—all this is history. But the satanic element in the poor Indian's character seems to have been irrepressible: in the midst of his triumphs, at the very moment of his greatest success, the saint was discovered to be a bitter mockery, a vain idol, and how he fell, and in his fall crushed his high priests and most ardent devotees— is it not written in all the journals of the year 1871?

THE HIDDEN RIVER.

II.

ORE than three hundred years ago, on a fair October day, when golden sunshine fell rich and glowing upon the sparkling waters and the gorgeous forests, a strange group of men stood in the far north of our country on the summit of a high hill, looking with wonder and with amazement at the grand sight before them. The central figure was a seafaring man—so said the weather-beaten countenance and the well-poised rest of the huge frame; but the dress was rich, the manner haughty, and from his eye flashed an intelligence that spoke at once of long, deep thought in days gone by, and of bright and glorious visions of the future. But who are those strange beings by his side, who look with stealthy glance at the strange form and mysterious ways of the great man? Their dusky skin, their savage weapons and rude covering betray the poor children of the soil, standing half proudly, half affrighted in the presence of a stranger, in whom their instincts see the enemy, and their heart's faint apprehensions the future master.

The stranger was Jacques Cartier, the Master-Mariner

of St. Malo, whom King Francis I., king of France, had sent out a second time to explore the unknown Western World, and to find out its rich mines of gold and silver. He had once more entered that vast estuary, the mouth of the St. Lawrence, and, leaving his larger vessels behind, sailed boldly up the great river, till he reached a beautiful island lying in front of a lofty mountain. Here he found an Indian village, Hochelaga, and soon saw himself surrounded by the owners of the land, who came to gaze with marvel and with awe at the white man, in whose hands were thunder and lightning. He ascended the mountain, and, struck by its beautiful shape and commanding position, he called it the Royal Mountain, the Montreal of our day. And then he drank in with eager delight and prophetic vision the exquisite beauty and vast grandeur of the scene below him. There was the magnificent river, sending its rich tribute to the distant ocean, and lined on both banks with smiling prairies and shady forests. As far as the eye could reach, the rich soil, the luxuriant verdure, the abundance of game, and the very beauty of the landscape seemed to invite man to com and enjoy the boundless treasures of a virgin land. But, as he looked westward, his penetrating glance fell upon the rippling waves as they danced merrily in the lingering light, and beyond the foaming rapids upon a vast sheet of water glowing in deep bloody red, and stretching apparently without limit towards the setting sun. Surprised and wondering he turned to the painted chief by his side, and uttered a few short words. Had he really already discovered the great open sea that should afford Europe a pathway to distant Cathay, and by a short route bring the treasures of the Indies to the harbors of France? Then came the answer, slowly, solemnly: "That river at your feet has passed through three great seas, and beyond these lies another sea of fresh water, which has no bounds; and still farther towards the setting sun is another great river, which flows to the land from which the sweet winds of the southwest bring us health and happiness, and where there is neither snow nor ice."

Such were the first faint rumors of the distant Mississippi, that ever fell upon the ears of a Christian. A vague longing to see this marvellous world of ocean-lakes and gigantic rivers filled the heart of the bold sailor, and, thanks to his eloquent words and glowing accounts, spread throughout fair France, till knight and monk, lord and varlet, vied with each other in fearless effort and ready sacrifice to penetrate the great mystery. Pious Jesuits gave their lives to raise the Cross of Christ in the wilderness, and haughty nobles stooped to become hewers of wood and drawers of water in order to secure a New France to their great sovereign. Providence granted them the coveted boon, and France can inscribe upon the scanty roll of her discoveries the proud claim of having first explored the interior of the New World, and to have revealed to the world the great mystery of the Hidden River.

It was fortunate for the French discoverers that it is

a national trait of their people to act impetuously, upon the impulse of the moment. For already, rivals had appeared in the Spanish navigators of that day, who threatened to be before them in the eager race. In the great ports of the world, and at the courts of many a sovereign, faint reports would be heard of a bold sailor, who, as long ago as 1528, had undertaken the conquest of all the lands on the northern shore of the Mexican Gulf. Fortune, however, had been against him; he had died, and storms by sea and famine by land, disease and death, had made sad havoc among his followers, till only five survived. These were made captives by the very men whom they had come to capture, but after four years' slavery they escaped and boldly struck inland. Here they met Indians who had never yet beheld white men; and being looked upon and revered by them as supernatural beings, they availed themselves of the prestige to cross the continent from ocean to ocean. Their leader was Cabeza de Vaca (lowhead), and his name, repeated by many a stammering tongue in France and in England, was, for generations, a by-word of fearful perils endured and of strange discoveries made in distant America. There is no doubt that he must have seen the Great River, as yet unnamed; that he must even have sailed for some distance on its turbid waters; but his narrative makes no mention of the fact; and the cautious policy of the Spanish Government withheld whatsoever information it may have obtained : the river was still unexplored, and even in official dispatches alluded to only as the *Hidden*

River. But, as if in defiance of all such jealous precautions, the "Inland Sea," as it was often called, soon rang its fame once more in the ears of all Europe, and though the words fell hard and heavy upon all who heard them, accompanied by the death-knell of a great and glorious hero, they only gained new attractions and greater lustre by the sad tragedy, and filled the imagination with new visions of increased splendor.

A former companion of Pizarro, Ferdinand De Soto, had longed for years to renew the life of reckless peril and surpassing glory which awaited the bold adventurer on the shores of the New World. Allured by mysterious rumors of vast treasures hid in the forests of the continent, and misled by lying reports of treacherous Indians, he had abandoned the governorship of the rich Island of Cuba, had landed in Florida, and marched his faithful followers—the largest army of Christians ever yet seen in the New World—from the shores of the Atlantic far into the wilderness. Led by a captain of dauntless energy, his troops became invincible; in vain did the elements shroud the chaste beauty of the virgin land in veils of mist and rain; in vain did pathless mountains rise in their way, and swollen rivers angrily stop them in their progress;—they were men, and felt and proved themselves masters of all nature. In vain did the natives try to impede their march by cunning and by force: they easily triumphed over rude and ill-directed masses of half-armed savages, and soon learnt to be wary and watchful. Their horses fell in forest and field; their heavy cannons stuck fast in mud and mire; their very weapons were lost or destroyed in many a skirmish and conflagration, and their numbers were sadly diminished, but they only closed their ranks in silence, and with sturdy minds and stout hearts pressed close after their indefatigable leader. But what all the powers of nature and all the passions of man had failed to accomplish, was at last brought about by the death of their noble chief.

They had marched for months, ever straining their wearied eyes for a gladsome sight of the Hidden River, when, on a bright summer morning in June, 1541, the coveted goal was at last reached. As their foremost horsemen broke from the forest and eagerly galloped up a gentle slope, they found themselves suddenly upon a steep bluff, and at their feet rolled the waters of a mighty river, such as their eyes had never yet beheld in this world. Their hearts were too full of gratitude, we are told, to utter words of thanks, or even of wonder; they halted and gazed at the great mystery till their eyes overflowed and their pent-up feelings escaped in one great cry of delight. Even then they knew not how to call the gigantic stream; the Great River it was to them for a time, and as such it appears in the first account of the expedition which we owe to a Portuguese adventurer, who seems to be himself involved in the mystery which still shrouded the river, and is quoted by Hakluqt (1609) only as a "Gentleman from Elvas." Nor is it quite certain whether De Soto himself, or earlier historians, gave to the river the next name it bears, Rio del Espiritu

Santo, under which it is already entered in a map drawn up in 1521, to establish Garay's claim to its discovery. "The river," says the Gentleman from Elvas, "was almost half a league wide; if a man stood still on the other side, it could not be discerned whether he was a man or no. The river was of great depth and of a strong current; the water was always muddy; there came down the river continually many trees and timber, which the force of the water and stream brought down (Hist. Coh's. of La., II. p. 168). Two hundred canoes, laden with armed and painted Indians, came dashing down the current to greet the new-comers; the chieftain's boat, gorgeously apparelled, led the gay procession, and every canoe was bright with waving plumes and clanging shields. The delighted Spaniards eagerly drank in the rare sight; they looked with fierce covetousness at the populous towns that dotted the country, and at the mighty river that was to be their key to the land of gold. For many months they sailed on its waters and marched along its banks, wintering within sight of the river. But another great tragedy was approaching, to add new gloom and new mystery to the annals of the Hidden River. In the following spring De Soto fell sick, refused to yield to the advice of friends and the promptings of nature, and succumbed. Who can tell the poignant grief, the overwhelming sense of desolation that his death must have caused in the hearts of his followers, his faithful friends? Decimated by disease and incessant warfare; stripped of all comforts, of their wonted food, and even of scanty clothing; weighed down by grief for the lost ones, and by sore fears for the future, they were suddenly robbed of their leader, who had watched over them with fatherly care, encouraged them by his example, and cheered them by his indomitable spirit. The happiest issue, the brightest hope they dared to anticipate was to float down the mysterious river through hosts of hostile nations, to be carried, they knew not whither,—to the Vermillion Sea in the Pacific Ocean, or to nearer gulfs and friendly harbors. But first they had to perform their last solemn duty to their beloved chieftain; to secure his remains against the fierce hatred and bitter revenge of the Indians. At a place not far, probably, from the Lower Chickasaw Bluffs, they cut down a gigantic oak tree, carefully hollowed out the immense trunk, and in this strange coffin deposited the body of their great leader. Then, on a dark and gloomy night, with the cross leading them onward, and unspeakable grief in their hearts, they marched in solemn procession to the river-bank; not a word was heard save the low chanting of the priest; the very voices of nature seemed to be hushed, and only the steady, unceasing surge of the sullen waters filled the air with its low murmuring sounds. Thus they reached a tongue of land jutting out into the river, and forcing it to narrow its channel and to deepen its bed, and here, in a place where the waters were nineteen fathoms deep, they deposited all that remained of their great chieftain. to rest there, safe from the scent of brutes and the passions of men, till his soul was to reawaken on the banks of "a pure river of water of life." Thus the discoverer of the Mississippi sleeps beneath its waters, adding another mystery to the many that give the Hidden River such strange charms in the eyes of philosophers and historians. For Spanish jealousy continued to preserve a rigid silence about all that had been discovered; the very place of the first sight is not accurately known, and the anxiety of Spain to preserve the integrity of its claims upon the whole of America, based upon the Bull of Pope Alexander VI., of 1495, contributed to increase, by fair means and foul, the mystery which for many a generation yet shrouded the Hidden River from the sight of man. Even Iberville, the daring Canadian sailor, who, after discovering the mouth of the river in 1699, had sailed up some little distance, was dismayed by its vast size and ominous fame, and, with faint heart, gave up the effort and returned to France without having solved the great question of the river that still remained to him, and to the world at large, the Hidden River.

It was left to a very humble countryman of his, a mendicant monk of the order of St. Francis, to hand down his name to posterity as the first European who is certainly known to have discovered and explored the larger portion of the great river. This was Father Marquette, a native of Picardie, and one of the most illustrious missionaries of France. A Recollect, as his special order was called, he had devoted himself to the conversion of the Indians, exchanging the comforts of European life and bright prospects of a brilliant career in the Order of

Jesuits for the hardships of Indian wigwams and a martyr's crown of thorns. In his western home at Mackinaw he heard much of the great river and the countless nations of Indians that dwelt upon its banks. His heart burnt with a holy zeal to rescue them from eternal ruin, and though eminently useful among the Hurons, who loved and obeyed him like a father, he expressed his readiness to leave his newly-won home "to seek new nations toward the South Sea, who are still unknown to us, and to teach them of our great God, and to visit the great river in order to open the passage to so many of our fathers who have so long awaited this happiness." What touching humility, what burning zeal, in these simple words! Patiently he waited for long years, till worldly interest came to the aid of heavenly zeal. An enterprising fur-trader, Louis Jolliet, obtained permission from the governor and intendant of New France (Canada), to explore the great western river, and Marquette was ordered to accompany the party as missionary. After a long and tedious canoe voyage on smaller rivers, they sailed down the Mesconsin (Wisconsin) river, and found themselves at its mouth, gliding upon a gentle current into a vast inland sea. On the right rose a chain of lofty mountains, on the left lay fertile fields, and islands dotted the surface of the waters. The memorable day was the 17th of June, 1673, and was at once solemnly celebrated by the delighted voyageurs; a mass was held, a cross was planted, and the river called *Conception,* from the fact that the pious father had, from an early date, given up his whole life to the special veneration of the Immaculate Conception of the Virgin Mary, and fervently invoked the latter, as he touchingly tells us, "in order to obtain of God the favor of being able to visit the nations on the Mississippi River." The precise spot where the desired favor was first granted to him was, in all probability, near the present city of Prairie du Chien, and opposite to the town of McGregor, in Iowa. From here, he and his companions descended fearlessly the broad, unknown river, now past numerous islands with beautiful groves of cotton-wood, and then skirting immense plains on which moose and deer were browsing in peace, while strange animals swam across the river, and monstrous fish appeared in its waters. And all this time they were utterly alone, beholding no human face, and hearing no human voice in this appalling wilderness!

For a month the seven brave Frenchmen sailed down the great river in their frail canoe, seeing strange and weird wonders, meeting new tribes ate very turn, and ever holding their lives in their hands. But the cross they bore gave them strength of faith in the hour of peril, and the calumet, the magic power of which they had early discovered, secured them almost invariably a welcome among the Indians. It was only when they reached a village not far from the mouth of the Arkansas, which they called Akamsea, that more serious difficulties arose in the way, from the fact that they now encountered tribes speaking new and utterly unintelligible languages, and thus, having learnt that a few days' sail from where they were, the river surely fell into the Atlantic, they turned their bark up stream once more, on the 17th of July, and safely reached their northern home. It was fortunate for science that the humble discoverer was a man of high culture as well as of pious zeal, and the account of his journey, sent promptly to his superiors in France, but published only much later (1681, in Thevenot's Recueil de Voyages), is extremely graphic and surprisingly accurate. It is on a map attached to his " Narrative " that the river itself appears for the first time in print, and by its side the five great tributaries, the Wisconsin, Illinois, Missouri, Ohio, and Arkansas. Here also we read for the first time the much-abused name—Mississippi. It is true that Father Claude Dahlon, on a map of Lake Superior, which was published in 1670-1, entered already the words : " To the South flows the great river, which they call *Missisipi*, which can have its mouth only in the Florida sea, more than 400 leagues from here," but as the river itself is missing, the mere name cannot be valued highly. Father Alloues, also, had evidently heard the strange word, and his is, as far as known, the first recorded mention of the name. Speaking of certain Indian tribes he says : " They live on the great River, called *Mesipi;* " and in another place of the same official report he adds, · that a beautiful stream " leads to the great river named *Messi-sepy*, which is only six days' sail from here." (O'Callaghan *Jesuit Relations*, 1666-7, p. 106, and 1669-70, p. 92.) In a work of somewhat doubtful character (Carolana, by G. W. Gent, London, 1650, p. 113,) it is stated that a "Colonel Wood, in Virginia, inhabiting at the falls of James River, about 100 miles west of Chesapeake Bay, discovered, at several times, several branches of the great rivers, Ohio and *Mechasebe* in 1654." But here also the name is an empty sound, as no knowledge had yet been obtained of the river itself. It was only when Father Marquette had actually sailed for more than 2,000 miles on its broad bosom, and when its vast size and noble tributaries were fully appreciated, that the name of *Mississippi* became a reality. Men could now understand its meaning as derived from the two Algonquis words—*Missi*, great, and *Sepe*, a river. The almost countless varieties of forms under which the name appears are quite as much due to the violence done the original words by the dull ears and awkward tongues of Europeans as to the different dialects of various Indian tribes. Thus northern lips would call it *Meschasipi*, as quoted by Louis Hennepin, in speaking of the Illinois (Description de la Louisiane, p. 47), and southern tribes said *Meact-chassipi*, if we believe Du Pratz (Historie de la Louisiane I., p. 141), who blames his countrymen for corrupting the word into a French Mississippi. A later French writer, Dumont, falls back upon the barbarous form of *Mechassipy*, but under all these disguises we easily recognize the original *Missi*. Thus Michigan was at first known as *Missichiganen* (L'Hennepin II., p. 305); Lake Illinois was called by the Miamis *Mischigonong*, the great lake; and the famous central " home " of the Six Nations was in Iroquois called *Massaroomckes*, the great dwelling-place.

Michili Mackinack was formerly *Missili* Mackinae, and the Missouri bears the same imprint. It was only to the far South, among the Choctaws and the Chickasaws, that an entirely new designation was given to the Hidden River, and yet the meaning was the same. They called it *Oh-hinnah*, the great pathway of waters, a term which they substituted for the word River, which is wanting in their vocabulary.

And what became of the pious priest, the father of New France, as he has often been called ? He returned to his modest duties, carrying the glad tidings now to this and now to that savage nation, as his superiors ordered, or God's providence seemed to direct. Thus it was that in the sweet month of May, in the year 1675, he was making his way from Green Bay to his old friends at Mackinaw, not unconscious of his approaching end, and desirous to bid a tender farewell to his beloved children. But it was not to be. He had reached the mouth of a little stream falling into Lake Michigan on its eastern shores when he was overcome by fatigue and felt his end approaching. Erecting a small altar with his own hands under a melancholy pine-tree standing alone on the deserted strand, he said mass, heard the confessions of his companions, and then retired to his humble bark-cabin in the woods. Here he fell asleep never to awake in this world. Two canoemen, his only companions, dug his grave in the sand, and thus he went to his rest from his weary wanderings and incessant labors. But he was too dear to his red children to be left on that distant shore.

Two years afterwards his own flock came in large numbers, disinterred his remains, and prepared them for burial after Indian manner. They then placed them in a canoe, and a mournful flotilla sailing in its wake escorted them homewards ; here and there other tribes joined them ; from every bay and bight more canoes shot out to meet the solemn procession, and when at last they approached Mackinac, the lake and the heights and the welkin sang with the mournful chant arising from the waters. The little bark-box that held the sacred remains was deposited in a small vault of the church, and there, we are told, " he reposes as the guardian angel of the Ottawa mission."

But his grave was not, on that account, forgotten. The place is, to this day, pointed out to the traveller on the banks of the little river which now bears his name, and many a blessing is invoked upon the memory of the great missionary. "When the storms of the lake swept over the Indian's frail canoe, he called upon the name of Marquette, and the wind ceased and the waves were still," we read in the Nouvelle France (VI. p. 21); and the author tells us in his letters (Charlevoix, Letters, etc., II. p. 96) an apparent miracle which he witnessed. It was fifty years later when he visited the sacred spot, and to his great amazement he found that the waters had forced a passage for themselves at the most difficult point, cutting through a bluff rather than cross the low-lands, where he still saw the grave of Marquette !

It is almost painful to turn from this noble type of modest greatness and judicious zeal to the next visitor of the Great River, Father Hennepin. The second European who sailed on the waters of the Mississippi, he marred the interest and jeopardized the value of his important discoveries by boundless vanity and reckless exaggeration, making himself remembered, as Bancroft says, "not merely as a light-hearted, ambitious, daring discoverer, but also as a boastful liar." He might well have rested contented with the glory of having been the first Christian who ever ascended the great river from the mouth of the Illinois to the Falls of St. Anthony, and of having discovered a large part of the *Meschisipi*, as he frequently calls it; but his desire to astonish the world and to eclipse the fame of La Salle, led him to publish, in 1697, a description of Louisiana, in which he claimed to have also descended the river to its mouth. Strangely enough, the vivacity of his style, the accuracy of his descriptions, and the minuteness of detail imposed upon critics for centuries, and it was only in our day, and thanks to the unerring judgment of an American historian, that the imposition was discovered.

In the year 1682 the river, still a Hidden River to the world at large, assumed once more a new name. A French adventurer, once a Jesuit, then a fur-trader in Canada, and now a nobleman, bearing the title of an American domain, had his imagination excited by the reports of Marquette's discoveries, and determined to explore the Hidden River to its mouth. The authorities in France encouraged him in his enterprise, and he returned to this country with ample authority and valuable assistance to carry out his great plan. But once more the magic charm, which for a long time seemed to protect the mystery of the great river, threw countless obstacles in his way; friends forsook him, creditors abused him, and his ship with its rich freight disappeared on the northern lakes. Nothing daunted, he started in a frail canoe, reached, on the 2d of February, 1682, the banks of the Mississippi, and boldly ventured upon the appalling "wilderness of waters." Grateful to the minister, who had encouraged him when others smiled at his enthusiasm, he call the river the *Rivierè Colbert*, bestowing the name of the minister's son, Seignelay, on the Illinois River. Then he sailed down the whole length of the mighty river, the first European beholding the beautiful regions south of the Arkansas, till at last he reached the far-off mouth of the river, and thus completed the work his predecessors had left unfinished. There, on the 9th of April of the same year, he solemnly took possession of the whole vast valley watered by the great river and its gigantic tributaries in the name of his master, the King of France. Erecting a cross, with the arms of France, near the place where the waters of the gulf mingle with those of the river, he declared on a leaden plate, deposited in the earth, that "Louis the Great, King of France and Navarre reigns," and for him took possession of Louisiana. The name of the country was not now used for the first time, for it occurs already in Father Hennepin's account, which was printed in the same year, and must therefore have been in use before. (Charlevoix,

THE HIDDEN RIVER. 49

Nouvelle France, I., p. 464.) But the Hidden River was hidden no longer; its entire course had been explored and was speedily made known to the world. Hennepin still spoke of it as *Colbert*, saying "There are no Englishmen at the mouth of the River *Colbert*" (Nouvelle D´couverte, II., p. 310), and "Father Marquette found that he would have to look for some other river, besides River Colbert, that discharges itself into the Mar Vermejo, or the Caliphomian Gulph." (II. 348.) But now the majesty of the river, displayed in its full length, seemed to call for new honors, and thus it appeared now as River *St. Louis*, a name which it long retained. Although the "First Establishment of Faith in New France," in 1691, still speaks of the River Colbert, following probably, the example set by Joutel in his Journal, and even, once at least, by Father Hennepin, it was the *St. Louis* in Dumont and far into the eighteenth century. The former, taking the cue from the Memoires du Ch. de Tonty, states that "the River St. Louis has its source West of Canada, in the country of the Issatis, explored by Mr. Davén with Father Louis, a Recollect, four other Frenchmen, and two Illinois Indians, sent by de la Salle."

The Hidden River exacted the usual penalty from the daring discoverer;—De Soto had died in sight of the goal; Marquette lay buried in the wilderness, and La Salle fell by the hand of the assassin in a remote corner of Texas. Thus were the hands punished that dared to draw the veil from before our own Image of Sais.

Nor are the various disguises under which the Hidden

4

River appears in the annals of our continent, at an end yet. Charlevoix speaks of savages who call it *Malbouchia*, and there is a statement on record that the natives spoke to Iberville of the Mississippi by that name; but the word is too evidently French in form and in meaning to be charged to Indian idioms. Another name, *La Palissade*,' bestowed upon it by the Spaniards, was readily understood by the same Iberville, when he examined the mouth of the river in February, 1699, and found it thickly set with trees, which the fierce current was incessantly tearing away and replacing, thus forming a real and most dangerous palisade (Charlevoix, Nouv. Fr. II., p. 255). As the designation applied, however, to the mouth of the river exclusively, it never became popular, and with the name of *Barbancha*, mentioned by Dumont (Memoires Historiques de la Louisiane I., p. 3), soon disappeared from public records.

A similar fàte seems to have controlled the names of its great tributaries. The earliest mention of the Wisconsin, well-known to the French, who were quite at home on its waters, occurs on Thevenot's map accompanying Father Marquette's narrative, where it is called *Missiousing*. In the narrative itself, however, it appears regularly as *Mesconsin*, and the probability is great that this was originally intended for *Mescousin*, especially as Father Marquette also speaks of a River *Miskousing*. The Illinois was originally so-called from the name of the great Indian nation that lived mainly on its banks, because through it lay the direct route to the Illinois villages which Father Marquette was the first to visit. Joutel, in his Journal, speaks of them as the *Islinois*, but this is evidently the result of careless writing. They called themselves proudly the *Lenoré-Lenapé*, men of full age, in the vigor of their strength, and are quoted as such by La Salle, Joutel, and Hennepin. The latter calls them, at times, more correctly the *Illini*, "which, in the language of the nation signifies a perfect and accomplished man." (Nouv. Découv., p. 119.) The tribe was known as Miamis to the French, and as Delawares to the English; but among themselves they permitted no other designation but *Lenoré-Lenapé*. Heckewelder states in explanation of the term, that they claimed to be a nation from the far West, who had conquered all the eastern part of the American continent, and hence called themselves the original or true men. It has been ascertained that all their traditions point to a former home beyond the Mississippi, from whence their early ancestors came, conquering more ancient nations whose monuments are still scattered broadcast over the continent. Hence, also, more than forty powerful tribes called them reverently Grandfathers, in respectful acknowledgment of their ancient honors, while, in their turn, they rendered homage to the seniority of the Wyandots by calling them Uncles, and the Mohicans were honored with the title of Elder Brothers. Father Hennepin tried his best to deprive the useful river of its well-earned name. " I have named it, in the map of my Louisiana, the River *Seignelay*," he says, " in honor to the Minister of State of that name, who laid to the heart and took care of all the concerns of our discovery." (Nouv. Découv. II., p. 45.) But the effort was in vain; the name, never in actual use, soon disappeared from maps and State papers, and the *Illinois* retained its historic title.

Marquette speaks in his unpretending narrative of a village on the banks of the Mississippi, which he heard called *Oumisouri.* Here is, no doubt, the origin of the *Missouri* River, as it was called at a later period. For the Reverend Father himself speaks of it only by its Indian name, *Pekitanoni,* or the Muddy River, and enters it as such in his valuable map. La Salle seems to have heard of an Indian tribe, called the Massourites, but being more forcibly impressed by the number and power of the Osage Indians, and, like all Frenchmen, a very bad geographer, he boldly christened the river the *Osage* or Ozage, and as such it appears in Dumont, where it is mentioned as "the boundary line of Louisiana on that side." (Mém. Hist. de la La. II., p. 281.) It is not apparent why it should have been spoken of as the River *St. Philippe* in the proclamation of Louis XIV., which granted the colony of Louisiana to Crozat, in 1712, nor does the name appear elsewhere. The *Yellow River* of Dr. Daniel Coxe seems to be but a delicate substitute for the Muddy River of other writers, and has also disappeared from books and charts. Of all the great tributaries of the Mississippi, however, the Ohio has been forced to bear the greatest variety of names, and yet it is most interesting to observe how its great beauty has invariably remained triumphant in the great contest. There is little in the uncouth word *Ouabouskigon* to remind us of more familiar terms, and yet it is the first feeble effort to pronounce and write down the name which serves as a basis to our modern Wabash. Father Marquette, calling it in one place the *Waboukigon*, says elsewhere : " The Ouabous-kigou, which runs into the Mississippi in the latitude of 36 degrees N.L." (Narrative II., 341.) The name was gradually softened down into the *Houabache* and *Ouabache* of Joutel (Journal, p. 322), and the *Oubachi* of Kip's Jesuit Missions. At that time, it appears, the river was called thus throughout its whole length, although Dumont already tells us that it had " two branches, of which one is called the Ouabache, and the other the *St. Jérôme.*" (Mém. Hist. II., p. 294.) This seems to have led to endless confusion, as in the proclamation of Louis XIV., of the year 1712, in which again, the Ohio itself is called the River *St. Jérôme.* It became, however, soon known that the Wabash was but a branch or tributary of the *Hohio*, as Father Hennepin calls it, after the manner of the Iroquois. (Nouv. Découv., p. 15.) In another place he calls it the *Oyo* or *Ouyo*, and elsewhere again, he speaks of "a great river, called *Hoio*, which passes through the country." The explanation of the Indian name was well known to the earliest explorers already, for Joutel speaks of the river as the *Belle Rivier* of the Iroquois, a river " exceeding beautiful, with perfectly clear water and a very gentle current." (Journ., p. 322.) The great beauty of the noble river seems thus to have struck the untutored children of the wilderness as forcibly as the new colonists, and, thanks to this impression, the simple, sonorous names, though sadly disfigured by the broad sound of the *i*, has safely come down to our generation. There was no slight danger once that the gentle, appropriate sounds should be exchanged for others of dire import; the constant conflicts on its banks during the first efforts at settlement of a newly-opened country, and a severe, savage struggle between rival tribes of Indians, gave to the whole region a most mournful aspect in the minds of men, and the *Bloody River* was thought a fit name for a stream, the waters of which had often and often been crimsoned with the blood of many races. But the contest was short, and as soon as the fields once more bore golden harvest, and homesteads arose on every hillside and by every brook, the blessings of peace wiped out the sad memories of by-gone days, and the river was once more the *Ohio*, the Beautiful River. The Indians also seem, at one time, to have thought of bestowing a new name upon the noble stream; for many years the Delawares and kindred tribes spoke of it as the *Alleghany*, a term meaning here, as in the case of the mountain range, merely fine or long. The name was soon appropriated to the river now known as the Alleghany, and thus, much unavoidable confusion was avoided. The Ohio escaped a still more invidious distinction—that of becoming the Northern boundary of the United States. During the negotiations of the Peace of Paris, the British Commission strongly urged this frontier line, and Benjamin Franklin, for reasons of his own, supported the enormous claim. Adams, however, and Jefferson, were violently opposed to such curtailment, little as the boundless value of the Northern lands could then be appreciated, and thus the calamity was averted. (I. Burnet's Ohio.)

The *Arkansas* River has its strangely accented name, evidently from the Indians, whom Father Marquette and Jolliet found at a village, which they called now *Akansea* and now *Akamsea*. They lived here amid Sioux and Chickasaws, we are told, and spoke a language entirely different from that of the Algonquin tribes, with which the French travellers were well acquainted. This difficulty seems to have appalled the latter, and on the 7th of July, 1673, they turned their bark homeward and sailed back without having seen the lower part of the river. Joutel also visited these Indians, and was greatly delighted upon his approach to the village to find there a tall cross, which his pious predecessors had erected. It was "a great comfort," he tells us, "to him and his companions, after so much fatigue and suffering," when they saw the great Christian emblem at *Accanca*, in the month of June, 1687. Father Membré is the first to spell the name *Akansas*, and it is by no means unlikely that the tendency of Americans to insert an inorganic *y* after an open *a* may alone have led to the present pronunciation. The place gains additional interest from the fact that it was probably not far from the Indian village of Guachoya, where the ill-fated De Soto had breathed his last nearly a hundred and thirty years before.

Still greater confusion reigned for long years in the minds of men concerning the last great tributary of the Mississippi. It was frequently confounded with the Arkansas, and at other times designated by the names of its principal branches. The first writer who mentions it, is the Sieur Joutel, in his Journal, and he speaks of it after the manner of all the early discoverers, as the River des Oumas—the Indians, who lived on its banks. They were, in all probability, the Maumee or Oumiami of other writers, since long afterwards, Dumont still calls the river by its ancient name, Rivierè de *Mâme* on des Oumas." (Mém. Hist., p. 37.) Its present title of Red River appears, however, almost simultaneously, for while Dumont calls it also Rivieré de la *Sublormier*, it is by other French writers referred to as the *Rivierè Rouge*, the *Colorado* of the Spanish. The red sand over which it flows, through a large part of its course, was too striking a feature to be overlooked, and hence the early preference for the picturesque name. The river furnishes us another evidence of the fact that on our continent also the French have signally failed in all attempts to establish permanent colonies; for while the great inland States, such as Kentucky and Ohio, were yet utterly unknown to the English, the Valley of the Mississippi was already enlivened by a chain of forts held by French garrisons. The Red River had its master as early as the year 1715, stationed in a fort, thirty-five leagues from its mouth, and controlling a number of powerful tribes in that remote region! But a few years only passed away, and not a trace remained of French rule.

The strange vicissitudes and romantic incidents which make the history of the Hidden River, during nearly a whole century, one of the most attractive features in the annals of our country, lend, at least, occasionally a like interest to certain localities on its banks. Thus, few of us can well help envying Father Hennepin the strange wonder and deep awe that must have filled his soul, when, after having been the first to behold the gigantic cataracts at Niagara, he was led to discover, in like manner, the great falls of the Mississippi. It must be borne in mind that they were far grander in those days than they are now: within the memory of men now living they have lost much of their height, and ere long, the rocky barrier that forces the river to plunge, fretting and fuming over the precipice, will be entirely worn away or removed by the hand of men. In those days, however, the falls were high and imposing—Hennepin speaks of fifty feet; the mighty river fell over the rocks in vast foaming masses, and the thunder shook the air for miles and miles. In silent admiration the bold explorer stood for a while gazing at the sublime spectacle, and then, in memory of the saint he had chosen to be the special patron of his daring enterprise, he named them the Falls of St. Anthony of Padua. The Indians, who then dwelt near the romantic spot, the Sioux, called the falls, in their musical language, *Owahmenah*, the Falling Waters, but the name passed away with the tribe. On a tree near the cataract the Franciscan monk engraved a rude emblem of the arms of France, and thus took solemn possession of the upper part of the great valley also in the name of his sovereign.

The falls were the natural end of his explorations, and he and his companions sailed down again, bent upon more discoveries. Unfortunately, they fell into the hands of savage Indians, who sadly ill-treated and nearly starved them; torture and cruel death even were threatened, and when the captives reached the broad expanse of the Great River, now known as Lake Pepia, a strange, weird scene served to give it an ominous name. The Indians had made a halt here, to consult on the fate of their unhappy prisoners: the council was divided, some inclining to mercy, while others were clamorous for massacre. In this dilemma, the cruel party, "those who were for murthering us," Hennepin calls them, resorted to a strange measure to obtain the consent of the others. During a long dismal night they wept profusely, loudly, incessantly, in order to move their milder-hearted companions by their tears of distress! Fortunately they did not succeed; mercy prevailed, and the lives of the brave Frenchmen were spared. But the *Lac des Pleurs*, the Lake of Tears, was forever engraven on the memory of the travellers, and as such it appeared for generations on every French map and chart of the Valley of the Mississippi.

Great St. Louis even, the Queen city of the West, had but a sad beginning. French settlers had sought new homes on the banks of the Great River, hoping to reap golden harvests from the rich bottom-lands and to gather precious peltry from the countless Indians around them.

Alas! the soil refused bread, but gave them fevers, and the natives preferred robbery to honest trade. The poor colonists were soon stripped of all their possessions, and, unable to till the land, exposed to cruel suffering and brutal ill-treatment. Their sorrowful fate may be read in the names of their homes. There was *Misère*, short and expressive, *Crevecoeur*, in token of broken hearts, *Vidépoche*, (now Carondelet, six miles below St. Louis,) speaking of empty pockets, and *Pain Court*, suggestive of short commons. A strange blunder of a great writer furnishes us with the connecting link between the last-mentioned name and the great city which is now the very emblem of exuberant wealth and marvellous progress. When Volney visited the West, and recorded his experiences there, he found that " St. Louis or Pancore (sic) had about 500 inhabitants, of whom five or six were rich." To the Frenchman himself, Pain Court had become evidently unknown in the anglicized Pancore of later days! The city had, however, then already begun its brilliant career; from a mere trading-post, favorably situated in the centre of large and powerful tribes, and on that account chosen, in 1763, by a French fur trader, Eaclède, it had rapidly grown into a town; the Spaniards then fortified it in 1780, and soon it fulfilled the hopeful predictions of the first settlers, who had foretold its future greatness. Nearly opposite the beautiful city, where smooth, rocky precipices rise like artificial works of fortification, and gladden the eye with their gentle slopes, glowing in the rich green of rare turf, stands Monk's

Hill, once the only convent of Trappists in this country. (Brackenridge, Louisiana, p. 274.) In the year 1806, the first of the silent brethren came over and selected the beautiful spot for their ascetic place of penance; soon other followers of La Trappe joined them, and a stately monastery arose on a lofty mound. But even as monks, the French failed to maintain their place amid the pushing, restless English, by whom they were surrounded on all sides, and already in 1813 the handsome building and the rich lands in the 'American Bottom,' which they had tilled with their own hands, were sold and abandoned by their austere owners. They returned to their native land, which, amid all its rich beauties, has no spot more lovely than the one they left, and ere this generation passes away, their memory will be lost in the West, and the land, where they once lived and suffered, will know them no more.

A strange river is the Mississippi in its wayward course down the great valley which it waters; as if conscious of a giant's power, it rushes headlong towards the sea, and, with a touch, moves aside all obstacles in its way. Here it cuts through a solid tongue of land in search of a shorter channel; there it spreads leisurely over a vast plain on the right or the left, forsaking its former bed; and at other places it sweeps away islands or lifts up the homes of men and carries them whithersoever it pleases. Such was the fate of two memorable towns, St. Geneviève and New Madrid. The former was the first town laid out in the State of Missouri, by French settlers from Kaskashia, who here erected large and profitable salt-works, and soon made their new abode the very picture of comfort and happiness. But a great flood occurred in 1782, the river rose, and ruthlessly swept away the whole town. Orchards, and a few ruins alone marked the spot, where the blooming village had once stood, in 1820. (Brackenridge, Louisiana, p. 229.) Since then, however, the town has been partly rebuilt, the memory of the *Année des Goux*, as the fatal year was called, is fading away, and men eat and drink, marry and are given in marriage—till the flood comes and destroys them all once more? Still sadder was the fate of New Madrid, for the Mississippi now literally flows over the houses of the ancient town, and the old grave-yard, with its touching memorials of long departed worthies, has apparently travelled from the State of Missouri to the State of Kentucky.[1] For, in 1811, there came a terrible earthquake,—the gigantic river rose in great perturbation, and by one vast effort swept away more than half of the whole country! No wonder that pious enthusiasts saw the signs of approaching dissolution in the disaster, and that many were swallowed up by the rising waters as they lay prostrate before their altars, imploring the aid of their saints and the mercy of the Most High.

The most illustrious Indian tribe, in what was once Louisiana, and by far the most faithful ally of the nation that so long owned its rich lands, were the Natchez. They appear first as *Nachië* in Father Membré's account of the river, on which they lived, and from that day the name assumed a thousand fanciful disguises, safely emerging at last in its present form. From their first meeting with Europeans, these brave and independent men seem to have inspired the new-comers with a feeling of esteem not void of awe, and whether in peace or in war, they always commanded the affection of their friends and the respect of their enemies. Inevitable fate, however, brought at last both parties face to face, and terrible wars ensued, during which, unfortunately, the savages often surpassed the warriors of France in valor, and the Christians exceeded the Indians in brutal cruelty. Upon a noble bluff overhanging the Great River, the French captain, Iberville, built in 1714, a strong fort on the very spot where, fourteen years before, his matchless foresight had induced him solemnly to lay the corner-stone of a city. The fort received the romantic name of Fort Rosalie, in honor of the fair Countess of Pontchartrain, but it was soon to be baptized in blood. The place had been carefully chosen, partly on account of its commanding position, and partly because in its immediate neighborhood lay the five principal villages of the Natchez, which could thus be easily held in check and maintained in faithful submission to the French Government. But the officers were haughty and licentious, the men intemperate and careless, and thus it came about that in a dark November night, 1729, the Indians suddenly overpowered the garrison and brutally massacred even the women and children. Scions of noble houses, pious priests, brave soldiers tried in bloody wars from early youth, and tender ladies fresh from the court of France —all were involved in the sad tragedy. Louisiana was mourning from distant ice-bound Quebec to the mouth of the river, and for years lamentations and heart-rending sorrow filled countless unhappy homes in the fatherland. There was little to comfort the bereaved in the revenge which was soon taken, though the national honor was restored and the Natchez ceased to exist. " A renowned captain, Perier de Salvert, brother to the Governor of the colony, marched, in 1733, an imposing force into the land of the Indians; he burnt their villages, defeated their armies, and at last took their great stronghold, an immense fastness west of the river. Those that were not killed on the spot, were carried in chains to New Orleans, and from thence sent as slaves to San Domingo. A few only escaped on the road, and found a refuge at Coosa; they were all that remained to bear witness of the former greatness of the valiant Natchez. Fortunately, the name was preserved from oblivion by being transferred to the settlement, which gradually sprang up around the ancient fort, and the beautiful city on the banks of the Mississippi, recalls to us the memory of the most illustrious and most formidable among Southern Indians.

One of those ready witted, rollicking adventurers, whose reckless courage and strange fate make the early history of New France read like a romance, had the good fortune of winning the favor of men high in power, and thus obtained a "concession," as it was called, wherever he might like to choose his abode. So he sailed up the river, merrily spending his time with a few boon companions, and leisurely looking out for some pleasant spot, not yet held by previous title, and promising a fair return for moderate labor, in rich harvests or precious metals. At last he found what he sought on a high bluff overhanging the river, on which a solitary cypress stood like a sentinel, ready to warn the unfortunate owners of the soil of the arrival of eager, invincible conquerors. He chose the beautiful hill with the rich bottom-lands at the foot, and built here, in 1722, the first house. The noble tree, with its prodigious size, its wide-spreading branches, which formed a vast baldachin on high, and its lofty trunk, rising clear from the ground to an immense elevation, and weird and woful with its red bark in the light of the setting sun, formed naturally the great landmark of the new settlement. A facetious comrade having suggested what a fine walking-stick the great tree would make, the jest was carried out, and the place, now the capital of a State, ironically called Red Stick, or *Bâton Rouge.*

Farther down, where the river bends suddenly around a projecting miniature cape, and then spreads out its dark waters till they assume once more the form of a lake, an odd name reminds us forcibly of the days when the Hidden River still fully deserved its mysterious name. This is the *English Turn.* Nearly two centuries ago, a quaint, restless Englishman, whose prominent share in the early history of our country would amply repay more thorough examination, Dr. Daniel Coxe, sent, upon his own account, two armed vessels southward on an exploring tour. One of these ships, a brigantine of sixteen guns, under a Captain Barr, was despatched for the special purpose of examining the mouth of the Mississippi, to take soundings in the passes that lead from the bay into the river, and to sail up as high as might prove expedient. The vessel had accomplished the preliminary investigations, and was proudly sailing up-stream, the happy captain enjoying the delightful sense of triumph in discovering a vast river and adding magnificent territories to the realm of his sovereign, when lo and behold! another armed vessel appears at the upper end of the apparent lake, and on its mast-head flies the white flag with the lilies of France! Great was the Englishman's disappointment, but greater still his rage, when the French commander, the great De Bienville, with haughty civility, informed him that the river and the banks of the whole magnificent country belonged to his master, the King of France and Navarre, and that no British vessel could be allowed to sail in these waters! There was nothing for it but to submit, and on that fatal day, the 20th September, 1699, the locality received the name of the English Turn, which it still bears in our day. It lies in *Plaquemine* Parish, a district so named from a grove of persimmon trees (plaquemines), which formerly stood upon the place where the first fort was erected; the French settlers having been struck by the vinous sweetness of the novel fruit.

The Great River leaves its last, and perhaps its richest, blessing to the State and the city, which formed, for so many generations, the centre of French political life in New France. The former, long known to English ears as part of *Carolana*, and still so-called by Dr. Coxe, in 1699, was from the beginning known to the French as Louisiana, bearing the proud name of the great Louis. Although Charlevoix claims the honor of thus naming it for La Salle (Nouv. Fr. I., p. 511), it is doubtful whether the word can be found in any work preceding Father Hennepin's Description of Louisiana, printed in Paris, 1683. It was in that year that three bold adventurers erected a cross in the name of the Church, and by its side, a stone column, in honor of their sovereign, and thus solemnly proclaimed to the amazed wilderness the right of Louis XIV. to rule over all the lands of America lying west of the Alleghany Mountains! Already in 1699 the first French settlers came over; Iberville was appointed Governor of the new colony, and Old Biloxi, at the mouth of the Lost River, was made the capital.

The choice of the first settlement soon proved to have been injudicious, and the seat of government was moved to New Biloxi. In the meantime, a few straggling huts had been erected on the Hidden River, at a place where it bent in the form of a half moon, and thus seemed to offer unusual advantages for traffic. On a fine summer day, in the year 1728, Bienville, the enterprising, energetic commander, the very soul of the colony, came down the river accompanied by some fifty persons, carpenters and galley-slaves, and stopped at this place, which his far-seeing wisdom had long since selected as the site of the coming city. Trees were at once cut down, fields were cleared, houses erected, and a fort added, and the new town named after the Regent of France, the Duke of Orleans. (Charlevoix, Nouv. Fr. III., 434.) Thus the crescent city received, as Bancroft says, "the name of New Orleans from the prince who denied God but trembled at a star." (Hist. III., 352.) As if evil omens must needs multiply on this occasion, the most unfortunate of modern financiers, John Law, who ruined the French in purse, as the dissolute prince did in morals, conceived a special fancy for the new colony, and in the same year sent out eight hundred men. They started from La Rochelle, under the auspices of the Mississippi Company, and reached their new homes only to learn, upon landing, that the gorgeous bubble had burst, their patron had fled, and their prospects were blasted. They scattered to the four winds, the large number of Germans among them alone remaining in and near the promised city, and thus adding a few new houses to the huts of the "voyageurs" that had come down from the distant land of the Illinois. The admirable judgment of Bienville soon proved not to have been at fault; the town grew in spite of fevers, overflows and hurricanes, and became already, in 1722, the capital of the new empire. Even then, however, the beginnings were but small as yet: the houses were built of cypress logs, the only church did not hold the increasing number of worshippers, and great was the joy of the colonists when a cargo of damsels was announced to be in the offing. They were the third load of girls sent out to supply the urgent wants of the settlers, and as they were all of good character and each endowed with a small chest to hold their property, these " Filles de la Cassette," as they were called, " had no time to be tired, for they were married instantly," says the quaint old chronicler.

The river, now no longer the Hidden River, but exulting in the proud name of the *Fleuve St. Louis*, after leaving the city, finally passes down to the gulf, half lost in marshes, sandy low-lands and impenetrable canebrakes. Far down, on its north-eastern pass, there rises the last landmark, a beacon, which has been pointing out the path to the weary and puzzled mariner ever since the year 1722, when the first *balise* (beacon) was erected there on piles, and a small fort was built in like manner, called the Poste de la Balise, to protect the entrance of the river. Below this last habitation the river may still be traced for some distance by the color of its waters, contrasting strongly with those of the gulf, and then it becomes once more, what it had been for nearly a century after its existence had been first ascertained, a Hidden River.

OUR FIRST ROMANCE.

III.

WHATEVER power we may possess to put ourselves, in imagination, in the place of others, and thus to realize, in some degree, what they may have felt and thought at certain times, no effort of our minds, no straining of our fancy can well bring home to us the sensations that must have filled the heart of the "Emperor of Virginia" when he was, at the age of sixty, for the first time confronted by men who came in floating and winged houses, and commanded the thunder and the lightning. Powhatan, as he was popularly called by the English adventurers, from the name of one of his residences, Paw't-hanne, the Falls in the Stream, had been a chief by inheritance, the head of a powerful, though not numerous, tribe, known by his own name, and roaming unchallenged over vast hunting-grounds in Wingandacoa. But ambition had early inflamed his mind, and he had become a conqueror of great renown, subjugating one tribe after another, until he knew no rival from the Blue Mountains in the West,

to the Blue Ocean towards morning. Unlike other chieftains, moreover, he held his lands by an unusual but safe tenure : in every part of his paternal domain and in every one of the newly-conquered districts he had dwellings abundantly large to receive him and his retinue, and amply stocked with provisions for his entertainment. Thus his power had increased and his fame had spread farther and farther, from year to year ; with wondrous tact and matchless skill he had succeeded in not only holding his sway undisputed over numerous tribes, more subtle and cunning than the Arabs of the desert, and spurning, in their independence, the very shadow of restraint, but he had actually united them, by the prestige of his valor and the power of his address, into one great union. To this new empire, far greater than that of King Philip of Mount Hope, and fully equal to the dominion of Tuscaloosa, the Black Warrior of the Mobilians, he had given his name, and thus it was that ruler, and nation and river, all bore alike the same designation. His fame rises in its vast range and unequalled power far above that of any other Indian monarch whose name has been recorded in our annals. He had, in the vast territory over which he ruled, by the mere terror of his name, no rival and no peer ; his nearest neighbors, the powerful confederacy of the Manakins and Manahoacks, trembled when he threatened to attack them, and the dread of the formidable Sachem was felt alike at the northern lakes and on the banks of the mysterious western sea, the Hidden River of the Spaniards. He was now nearly sixty years old, but still in the full vigor of manhood, and showing no trace of the great efforts he had made and the sufferings he had endured. Suddenly news was brought to him that strange men, with white faces and features half hid in bushy hair, had landed upon the coast, and were, even now, boldly pushing their boats up the great river. They had come in canoes as large as his most spacious houses, which glided over the waters without paddle or oar, by the aid of gigantic birds' wings, and kept concealed in their close hold the terrors of thunder and the power of lightning. His brave heart never quaked for a moment; but in his mind, no doubt, arose vague memories of ancient traditions and weird legends he had heard in his childhood, of white men who were to come from the rising sun and to conquer the land of his fathers. News spread fast among his brethren, and he had long since been told of efforts that had been made elsewhere by early invaders, from the days when the first fishermen appeared on the banks of Newfoundland to the year when De Soto marched his ill-fated army from the Atlantic to the Mississippi.

It was in this startling emergency that the manly form and venerable majesty of the great Indian hero appeared to greatest advantage. There were no poets and no historians to record the exploits of his youth and his manhood, which might have rivalled the deeds of eastern sheiks and Christian champions, but all the more striking is the splendor in which his sun set, and the deep indelible impression he made upon the haughty conquerors.

Cunningly guessing the true purpose of the new-comers, he received them with courtesy, but also with caution, and though fully determined in his heart to renew his youth, and to fight once more the most terrible enemy he had yet encountered, he allowed no word to escape and no act to be done that might betray his purpose. And thus he continued to the end, the only one of his race whose personal majesty was never violated by wanton insult, respected by those who knew him well, and dreaded by all whom he met as an enemy. The very men among the English who tried their best to make him feel his inferiority to European monarchs, and endeavored to profit by his simplicity and ignorance, were forced to acknowledge their defeat. Thus, a Captain Newport, the sponsor of Newport News of Virginia, went up to one of his residences once, to bring him rich presents from the "Queenes dread Majestie," hoping to impress him with the glory of his sovereign, and to drive a good trade for his private benefit. Captain John Smith, who knew the Indian and his race thoroughly, had in vain tried to dissuade the covetous Captain from making the visit and delivering the presents. He was fully aware that a basin and ewer, a bed and other furniture could be at best but curiosities for the stern old savage, and he foresaw, with instructive shrewdness, that the proposed plan of crowning the chief after the manner Old World monarchs was likely to end in dire dismay. But his eager countrymen had high hopes, and were so deeply impressed with the vast superiority of an English sailor over an Indian Emperor, that they insisted upon going through all the ceremonies they had planned. Here is their account of the scenes, which must have been disgusting to the noble old man, and irresistibly ludicrous to the unbiassed among the spectators. "His scarlet cloke and apparrell were, with much adoe, put on him, being persuaded they would not hurt him. But a foule trouble there was to mak him kneele to receive his crowne; he not knowing the maiestie nor the meaning of a crowne, nor the bending of knee, endured so many persuasions, examples, and instructions as tyred them hard. At last, by leaning hard on his shoulders, he a little stooped, and three having the crown in their hands, put it on his head—when by the warning of a pistoll the Boats were prepared with such a volley of shot that the king started up in a horrible feare, till he saw that all was right." . . . " Then remembering himself to congratulate their kindness, he gave his old shoes and his mantel to Captain Newport." On another occasion, when haughty Englishmen sent him word to come to great James city, to receive some presents which had been sent to him by their king, he replied in the simple consciousness of his dignity : "If your king have sent me presents, I also am a king, and this is my land. Eight days will I stay to receive them. Your father is to come to me, not I to him, nor to your fort." For, disguise it as we may, and poor, heathen savage though he was, he did not lack that divinity that " doth hedge a king." It shone forth in his acts, for he never did an ignoble thing, and stands ever before us in the simple majesty of a king, without a single act of tyranny or a moment's forgetfulness, and remaining to his death without a rival even among the gallant and adventurous men who then laid the foundation of a great and powerful country. It must have shone forth even in the tone of his voice and his personal appearance, for all who speak of him—enemies and supercilious judges though they were, agree in describing his dignity as imposing, and one of them adds pointedly : "When he listeth, his will is a law and must be obeyed ; not only as a king but as halfe a God they esteeme him. It is strange to see with what greate feare and adoration all these people (his Werowances or Huaker chieftains,) doe obey this Powhatan. For at his feete they present whatsoever he commandeth, and at the least frowne of his brow, their greatest spirits will tremble with feare."

Nor was he so entirely without the pomp and circumstance of real royalty as those seem to have imagined who have written about him as a "poor Indian." He had, as we have seen, a number of stately residences in various parts of his dominion, and some of these were not only of imposing size, but richly adorned. His principal residence seems to have been at Weroworomeos, a word simply meaning the Werowance's House, the same as the Wricacomacs of Maryland and Roger Williams Sachimma-comocko, the Sachem's House, which E. Winslow, in his Good News from New England, spoke of as, "Sachims-Comacs, for so they call the Sachem's place." It was built on the banks of the York River, where it broadens out into a vast estuary, and here he dwelt in barbaric state and splendor. It was to this place brave Captain Smith was brought by his captors, and here his life was saved by the most romantic incident in our early history. The place is still pointed out to the curious traveller, who is sure to visit Powhatan's chimney, a ruin built of the shelly conglomerate which abounds in the neighborhood, and now the only trace of the mansion erected for him by German workmen, whom the English settlers employed for the purpose, in order to please the grim old king. And he was pleased, for we are told, in the quaint words of a contemporary writer, how he would stand for hours, turning the key in the front door of his house, and, no doubt, wondering in his heart at the strange power possessed by the tiny instrument in his hand, to admit or exclude him at will. Known now as Timberuck Point, in Gloucester County, the place was long the ancient seat of the Mann family, and near by is Shelly, so-called from the immense heaps of oyster shells, which show that it must have once been a favorite resort of the Indians. Powhatan itself, the place called by the great chieftain's name, was little more than a hunting-lodge, on a beautiful eminence, overlooking James River, and a few miles below the present city of Richmond. Even here, however, all ceremony was not laid aside, for we are told that " About his person ordinarily attended a guard of forty or fifty of the tallest men his country affords. Every night, upon the four quarters of his house, are four sentinells, each from the other a slight shoot, and at every half houre, one from the corps on guard doth hollow, shaking his lips with his finger between them, unto whom every sentinell doth answer round from his stand." When the weary old king became disgusted with the trickery and treachery of his new and unwelcome neighbors, he sold this place to John Smith, who considered it justly the " strongest and most pleasant place he had seen in the country, and from this reason they called it Nonsuch." His plans to establish a colony here were however frustrated; although he could offer the settlers a number of " dry houses, near two hundred acres of land, cleared and ready to plant, with a Savage Fort, ready built," his subordinates were utterly unfit for the task, and the settlement was abandoned. The place became subsequently the seat of the Mayor, and is, to this day, considered one of the most beautiful sites on the magnificent river that once bore the great Indian's name.

At Orapakes, again, a residence farther inland, Powhatan had his vast store-houses, one of which seems especially to have attracted the attention of the English by its treasures and its quaint appearance. For on the four corners of this immense building, filled to the roof with " arms, skins, copper, pearls, and other valuables," stood four huge images as sentinels,—representing a bear, a dragon, a leopard, and a giant, " all made evile favouredly, according to their best workmanship." Kiskiask, another of the great monarch's favorite seats, underwent in its name a series of most strange variations; an Act of Assembly mentions it thus : " Be it also enacted and confirmed, that the parish of Chescake be called Hampton

Parish" (4th of Sept., 1632), and from thence the transition was easy enough to its popular designation as Cheesecake!

Now, this great king had a large family—not less than twenty sons and ten daughters, of none of whom any record is made in the accounts of the day, as the chieftain's power and dignity did not descend to his children, but to one of his brothers. Besides these thirty descendants, one daughter is mentioned by Swachey, " a young one, and a great darling," and finally she " whom Captain Smith intituled the Numparell of Virginia." In his famous letter to Queen Anne, the wife of James I., recommending the newly-married Indian princess to her kindness, he speaks of her as "the king's most dear and well beloved-daughter." Her name was originally Matoax or Matoaka, but her father's people always called her Pocahontas—so at least, it sounded to dull and inattentive English ears—for fear that the new-comers might learn to know her real name, and thus be enabled to inflict some injury upon their great darling. (Purchas IV., 1769.) How strangely this reminds us of the superstitions in olden times, when even Rome had her sacred and secret name of Valentia, and the name of the Lord could not be uttered by profane lips! The mysterious Matoax, for which no etymology has yet been found, because its sound was probably altogether changed by careless speakers, survives to this day in the land of the princess. Sometimes it is borne by persons whose parents cherish the old traditions of their native State; at other times by localities like the famous Matoax, one of the four original towns which afterwards combined to form the city of Petersburg, and a place full of interest to the patriot. For here John Randolph, if not born in the house, spent at least those early days of his boyhood to which he looked back so often in after life, with many a sigh and melancholy regret. Of the first years of the famous princess we know, of course, nothing; but when she first appears on the stage of the great and exciting drama that was then enacted in Virginia, she dazzles us like a meteor by the splendor of the romance and the sublimity of her heroism. We all know how gallant John Smith had fallen into the hands of the incensed Indians, and being forsaken by friends and allies, was about to be sacrificed in the presence of the king. He had been carried by his delighted captors with a rapidity that would alone have unnerved an ordinary man to Werowocomow, the distant residence of their monarch, on the northern side of York River, and with equal haste had been ordered to be brought to the palace. In the vast, but gloomy, ill-lighted house, where the stern, silent assembly of hideously painted warriors filled every nook and corner, the light fell from above, with startling clearness upon the grim old chief as he sat, in his imperturbably native dignity upon a couch of cunningly woven mats, and leaned against a pillow richly embroidered with pearls and precious white beads. Even thus sitting, he displayed his tall, well-proportioned form to advantage, and showed in his brilliant eye that, in spite of his age, there was much fire still left burning under the snow-white hair, and that muscles and sinews were strong enough yet to carry on wars and meet the most formidable of foes.

Immediately by his side sat his wives, for like King Solomon he had many, and around them two hundred of his highest courtiers, beyond whom were crowded the most renowned warriors of all the nations over which he ruled. In the dim distance, near the entrance, stood the small sturdy prisoner, unbound and unfettered, but well guarded by a thousand watchful eyes, sternly facing his fate, and yet, in all probability, not despairing of his life, for he had been in deadly peril too often not to know how many chances there are ever open to a truly bold and resolute man who keeps his presence of mind. The savage king casts a mere glance in his direction, and instantly two huge stones are brought in, and, with much labor and trouble, placed before his simple throne. Another glance from the bloodshot eye, and "as many as could lay hand" on the hated foreignér seize him, and drag him impetuously through the excited but immovable crowd; and ere he can well remember what has happened, he finds himself forced down, with his head lying on one of the stones, and a number of grotesque figures in terrible paint and apparel standing over him "ready to beat out his braines with their clubs." No doubt the bold captain then bethought himself of saying his last prayer, for he could not even look up and try the magic power of his eye that had so often, in like perils, done him marvellous service, nor could he raise his persuasive voice to enchain and soften, as of old, the hearts of his fierce enemies. But all of a sudden, a low, subdued cry of amazement escapes from a thousand wrought-up hearts; a slight flutter is heard, and in the next moment a young girl, a mere child, " got his head in her arms and laid her owne upon his to save him from death." When the prisoner glanced at her he beheld what must have looked to him little less than a vision; a fair, frail maiden, with her long black hair hanging loose around her child-like face, her eyes streaming with tears, and her whole attitude expressive of passionate entreaty and urgent prayer. It seems that even the stern old king had a secret tenderness for his favorite child, for it was Pocahontas, the " king's dearest daughter," who thus interceded, and with a gentle gesture of the hands he bade the executioners loosen their hold, and gave the captive to the tears of his child. The whole scene, dramatic as it appears in our stern matter-of-fact age, was still perfectly natural in all its simple features, and although Smith himself did not afterwards allude to it, caring little perhaps to remind his jealous rivals and restless detractors how he owed his life to the intercession of a child, we have a full and authentic account of all that occurred in a letter written by " Thomas Studley, the first Cape Merchant in Virginia, Robert Fenton, Edward Harrington, and John Smith," as recorded in Purchas.

From that day there was a bond of love between the renowned adventurer and the poor Indian princess, which death alone could break asunder. He never forgot that he owed his life, under God, to her tender heart and fearless intercession, and never spoke of her in the intimacy of his companions and friends, or in the formal appeal to the Queen's Majesty, except in terms of warmest affection and sincere respect. She returned his love with rare constancy from the day when she met his grateful look with blushing brow for the first time in her life, to that touching scene when, in a distant land and amid the very enemies of her race, who were fast conquering the land of her birth, John Smith would see in her only a king's daughter, and refused to let her call him father as heretofore. She said to him, with a well-set countenance: "I tell you then I will, and you shall call mee childe and so I will bee for ever and ever your countryman."

Nor was this a matter of sentiment only. With a woman's true and entire devotion to him whom her heart has once chosen as a master, Pocahontas henceforth loved the countrymen of Smith as she loved him. She became the earthly Providence of the infant colony, and watched over its wants and anticipated its perils with an energy and a perseverance which are astounding in a girl of her tender age. For although the year of her birth is unknown, we read of her as "a girl of tenne or twelve years old, which not only for features, countenance, and expression much exceeded any of the rest of her people, but for wit and spirit was the only nonpareil of the country." The annals of the early settlements are full of her acts of kindness and devotion. At one time, when Captain Ratcliffe, moved by the almost insane thirst of gain,

that seems to have possessed the English adventurers of
that day, had gone up into the Indian country, on Powhatan's fair possessions, and every one of the thirty or
forty men who had come with him to trade were murdered;
she rescued the only survivor, a boy named Henry Spilman, from instant death. He is represented to us as "a
young gentleman, well descended," who, having been
carefully protected by his patroness " among the Potowmacks," proved himself afterwards eminently useful to
Captain Argall. The latter had been sent by Lord de
la War, then Governor of Virginia, in an hour of dire
need, to obtain provisions from the Indians. Fortunately
he met the English youth, and by his acquaintance and
help " received such good usage from this kind people,
that his vessel was soon freighted with corn, with which
he returned to Jamestown," relieving the colony from the
imminent danger of starvation. At another time—in
1609—she accidentally discovered that a conspiracy had
been formed to destroy Jamestown and to exterminate
the English by one fell blow. There was danger in delay,
for the day for the surprise and the massacre was fixed
and close at hand; but undaunted, the brave girl escaped
from the jealous vigilance of her father, and on a dark
and stormy night she hastened, alone and unprotected,
through dismal forest and pathless morasses, to the place
where her friends slept in thoughtless security. At the
first news, the heart of the colonists sank within them
and they gave themselves up for lost; but when they
heard what the fearless Indian maid had done for them,

how she had ventured at midnight through a thousand dangers to warn them of their danger, " this so revived their dead spirits, especially the love of Pocahontas," that they armed themselves instantly, and thus defeated the plans of their subtle enemies.

How much she was yet of a child and given to childish pastimes, we see from a letter by Captain John Smith, who, always candid and even naively ingenuous, tells us frankly about her all he knows, without weighing the matter or thinking how his words might hereafter be misinterpreted by skeptic minds and less grateful generous hearts. " Jamestown," he says in his letter to the Queen, " with her wild train, she as freely frequented as her father's habitation, and she, next under God, during the time of two or three years, was still the instrument to preserve this colony from death, famine, and utter confusion. . . . The most and least I can do is to tell you this, and rather because of her being so great a spirit, however her stature." Carefully overlooking the noble tribute paid by the gallant adventurer to the Indian maiden, William Strachey, " first Secretary of the colony," in his " Historie of Travaile into Virginia Britannica," only remembered the girl's visits " with her wild train," and forthwith added to the account such details as would make it more attractive to certain m nds and less creditable to the princess. " Pocahanta, a well-featured, but wanton young girl, Powhattan's daughter, some tymes resorting to our fort, would get the boyes forth with her unto the marketplace and make the wheele, falling on with their handes, turning up their heeles upwards, whome she would follow and wheele so herself, naked as she was, all the fort over." If the account be true—and it must be admitted that there is no urgent reason to doubt the statement— she was probably a mere child, brought up in the wild woods, and utterly unfamiliar with the manners and customs of the English. As it is supposed that she was born in 1595, and Wm. Strachey was Secretary in 1610, this is at least possible. If she was older, so much the greater shame for the settlers, who encouraged the Indian boys and girls in such games and utterly forgot what they owed to themselves as well as to the maid, who must, in that case, have already been known to them as their kind friend and protector. Our great historian certainly did not credit the spirit of the secretary's remarks, for he mentions Jamestown as the place "where Pocahontas had sported in the simplicity of her innocence," (Hist. of the U. S. II., p. 227,) and thus follow the opinions entertained by Virginia's faithful chronicler, Burk, who speaks of her as one "whose soul Nature formed on one of her kindest and noblest models."

With all her efforts, and by all her ingenuity she could, however, naturally not always prevent misunderstandings between her own people and those whom she had chosen as her friends and her brethren, and her heart must have bled at the frequent butcheries which occurred in the next following years. At the same time, her father's patience seems to have been exhausted, or perhaps he was compelled, for reasons of state policy, to make an end to her frequent interpositions; to avoid disgrace, she disappeared for a time from the scene. Her friend, Captain Smith, having, in the meanwhile, left Virginia, she felt on that account also, less and less inclination to visit the colony, and thus she quietly withdrew to the home of a near kinsman, Iapasaw, who resided at Patawomeke. For two years she lived here in utter seclusion, sadly missing, no doubt, the society of those she had learned to appreciate, and sighing for another opportunity to become useful to the good people of the colony. She was not destined, however, long to remain here inactive and concealed from the world, for while she fancied that she had been forgotten by all and was living unknown among her kindred, she was, in reality, first and foremost in the thoughts of one of her foreign friends, and at the same time the subject of much speculation, and even of a bold conspiracy with the settlers themselves.

A year or two before, there had come to America, in company with Sir Thomas Gates, the Governor of Virginia, a young man of modest pretensions, but mentioned as "an honest and discreet" young Englishman, called John Rolfe. What position he occupied does not appear from the annals of the time, and it may well be doubted if he was anything more than one of the numerous "gentlemen" who then sought their fortune in the new Eldorado. He seems to have met with the Indian princess frequently at Jamestown, for John Smith tells us that he had "long before this been in love with Pocahontas, and she with him," but as yet no words had been spoken and no plans had been formed by the young man. Now, however, in the year 1612, a scheme was concocted by the colonists at Jamestown, which speaks little to the honor of the settlers and the views they had of the good faith due to the Indians and especially to her, to whom so many among them owed the preservation of their lives. This was nothing less than a plan to entice Pocahontas, by stratagem, back to Jamestown, and to hold her there as a hostage, in order to extort a number of special favors from her unfortunate father. Captain Samuel Argall, half pirate, half sailor, and afterwards known as Sir Samuel Argall, engaged readily to sail up the river to the place where Iapasaw lived, and to bring the poor Indian maid back with him to the fort. John Rolfe volunteered to accompany him in this expedition, though there is no reason to suspect that he now or thereafter speculated upon the influence he might gain over the young girl, and through her, over her father, the king. The treacherous plan succeeded beyond expectation. A copper-kettle was the price paid for the Emperor's daughter, and for this precious article Iapasaw and his rascally wife betrayed the child of their chieftain into the hands of the enemies of their race. On the pretext of an eager curiosity to see Argall's vessel, they proposed to their unsuspecting guest a visit to the strangers. As soon as the poor girl was in the cabin, she was informed of her captivity, "whereat the old Jew and his wife began to howle and cry as fast as Pocahontas," in order to make her believe that they were innocent of the betrayal, and then they hurriedly left the boat, carrying with them the bright shining copper-kettle. The poor prisoner, overcome with surprise and grief, was carried down to Jamestown, and messengers were sent at once to her father to propose negotiations for her exchange. But much as Powhatan loved his child, he was too wise to be caught in the snare, and sternly refused to do anything for her release. In the meantime a great change had been wrought in the gentle captive ; the wild, wanton girl of former days had grown up into a quiet, dignified maiden, and now Christian influences were brought to bear upon her, while at the same time her heart's deepest feelings were for the first time aroused.

The minister of Bermunda Hundred, the Rev. W. Whitaker, a man of eminent piety and rare good sense, saw the golden opportunity that was thus offered to him and at once discreetly but zealously, set to work to " win a soul for Christ." The early influence of her intercourse with Captain John Smith seems to have prepared the way for his kind words and gentle teachings, and he soon had the joy to receive her into the church of which he was so faithful a shepherd. All accounts agree that she was well instructed in the great truths of Christianity, and her whole life afterwards proved that they had sunk deep into her heart and changed her whole nature. This change was so striking that even at that time the letters of Sir Thomas Dale, the Lieutenant-Governor, and of the pious minister himself overflowed with expressions of wonder and gratitude. One of the later letters, dated

June, 1614, refers to these days, saying: "How careful they were to instruct her in Christianity, and how capable and desirous she was thereof; after she had been sometime thus tutored, she never had desire to go to her father, nor could well endure the society of her own nation ... and she openly renounced her country's idolatry, confessed the faith of Christ, and was baptized." She received in baptism the name of Rebecca, and became henceforth known as Lady Rebecca in acknowledgment of her rank as a king's daughter.

At the same time the young, enthusiastic Englishman improved his opportunity to win her affections, and though long too timid and bashful to confess his love, at last made a touching appeal to his friend and patron, the Lieutenant-Governor of the Colony, in a letter still extant. In words full of passion and all aglow with ardent admiration he acknowledges his love, and humbly asks permission to address the princess, and, if she should consent, to make her his own. Here again not a trace of selfish views or mercenary hopes is to be discerned. The letter was so evidently the expression of his true feelings, and his whole subsequent conduct proved so fully the earnestness of his attachment, that Sir Thomas Dale says: "the true affection she constantly bare her husband was much, and the strange apparitions, wild passions he endured for her love, as he deeple protested, was wonderful." In another statement we are told that "her affection to her husband was extremely constant and true, and he, on the other hand, underwent great torment and pain out of his violent passion and tender solicitude for her." (Stith Va. p. 132.) There was most assuredly too much of stern reality and of truthful simplicity in the colonial life of those days to allow us to look in such descriptions for romantic exaggeration or deliberate misstatements. There is no evidence whatever to be met with in the life of the two lovers, that Master John Rolfe wooed Pocahontas for any other purpose than that of simply making her his beloved wife.

The Governor's assent was given, and in his own house at Varina the happy lovers were united in the month of April, 1613. It must have been a strange and striking scene when the two representatives of the Old and New World thus stood side by side to utter mutual vows of love, and thus to typify unconsciously the new bond that was gradually to connect the two great continents with each other. There stood the simple, manly form of the fair young European, simple and unpretending, but every inch, as the Governor said, "an honest gentleman, and of good behaviour," and by his side, her hand in his, the dusky daughter of America, showing in her high cheek bones, her rather gloomy face and her lanky hair, as her portrait painted in London presents her to us, the characteristics of another race and another world. But although even her most ardent admirers have to admit that she never could have been a beauty, according to our ideas of beauty, there was, we are told, a wonderful charm in her face, which was not due to regularity of features or brilliancy of complexion, but solely to the nobitity of the soul that shone in every line. Her brilliant eyes, her winning smile, the sweet simplicity of her whole expression were irresistible, and won all hearts from the queen on her throne to the maid in the cottage. By the side of the groom stood his friends and countrymen in the rich costumes of the day, some in armory, some in courtly apparel, and before him, in unpretending dignity, the Rev. W. Whitaker in his gown and surplice. But who are those dark and strange forms that have come gliding in like dismal shadows flitting over a sunlit landscape, even while the attention of all the bystanders was riveted upon the pale bride and her fair English friends? They are decked in all the barbaric splendor of the sons of the forest, in gaudy paint, and covered with quaint strings of oddly mixed beads, and teeth and claws. After a while the colonists recognize in them Opahisco, a younger brother of Powhatan, the bride's father, with two of his sons, whom the great king has sent on purpose "to see the manner of marrying, and to do in their behalf what they were required to do for confirmation of it as his deputies." Surely, the grim old warrior must have had a delicate perception of what was proper and expedient on such an occasion, to imitate from pure instinct, and yet so closely, the usages of older nations and the ceremonies observed in other countries.

As, however "the course of true love never did run smooth," we are interrupted at this moment of apparent happiness and bliss by the cold-blooded statement of

William Strachey, before mentioned, that " Pocahunta, using to our fort in tymes passed, was married to a private captain, called Kokoum, some two years since." He even enforces his assertion by repeating it elsewhere in the words : " She lived as wife to another settler before John Rolfe." But his statement stands alone, unsupported by any evidence whatsoever, and is neither mentioned nor referred to by any other writer. It is hardly to be presumed that, in the multitude of notices concerning the great Indian princess, and her subsequent brilliant though short career in England, this fact alone should have escaped the attention of all other contemporary authors. Nor is it probable that the Governor's evident interest in John Rolfe's suit, or Captain John Smith's unfailing attachment to Pocahontas, should have ignored so remarkable an event. What is more likely, on the contrary, than that another child of the king's, perhaps the very daughter referred to as " a young one and a great darling," should have before this married an Englishman? Or, if that be not admissible, it may be fairly presumed that Kokoum was the Indian name of John Rolfe himself, and hence the two were one and the same person. For nothing was more common in those days than for those who wrote on Indian affairs to be hopelessly misled by the confusion of names. The dull, untutored ears of the common English settlers were little able to discern the delicate sounds of new and utterly strange idioms; they repeated them, no doubt, to the best of their ability, but that ability was very feeble indeed, and the trouble will be fully realized by all who have ever been called upon to repeat the more difficult sounds of foreign languages. Besides, it was the constant habit of the Indians to bestow their own names upon the leading men in the English colonies. The Governor of Canada was to them always Ormontio or Onondio; the Six Nations called every Governor of Maryland Tocaryhogan, the man living in the honorable place; the Governor of New England and New York were known to them as Corlaer, after one of the early Dutch settlers; and William Penn had even a punning name, being called Onas—the pen. The same custom prevailed in Virginia, where an Englishman appeared in the Powhatan dialect as Tassantasses, and William Strachey himself calls Pocahontas Amonate, a name which is not mentioned anywhere else. Even if he did not purposely misapprehend the matter, he may, therefore, very easily have been misled by this variety of names, and fancied that Kokoum and Rolfe were two different persons, as well as Pocahontas and Matoax.

After her marriage the Indian girl made more and more rapid progress in all that became her new station. " By the diligent care of Master John Rolfe, her husband, and his friends, she was taught such English as might be well understood," and she soon put her newly acquired knowledge to good purpose. " For she promptly acquired, with a woman's ready instinct and an ardent desire to please her husband, the habits of European life, till her old friend John Smith, could write of her to his queen ; " she was become very civil and formal after our English manner." In the meantime her father had also gradually forgiven the terrible offence, when his beloved daughter was forcibly torn from him, and when several gentlemen had been sent to him at Pamaonke, one reports that " he offered me a pipe of tobacco and then asked me how his brother, Sir Thomas Dale did, and his daughter, and his unknown sonne, and how they lived, loved and liked ? " When the ice was thus broken, new efforts were made to bring about a perfect reconciliation, and John Rolfe himself accompanied an embassy sent to Powhatan, and was kindly received.

Thus, improving daily, and enjoying great happiness, bride and groom lived together " civilly and lovingly," till their friend and patron, Sir Thomas Gates, resolved to return to his native land, and an arrangement was made by which the young couple were to accompany him to England. Once more Captain Argall appears upon the scene, but this time in the friendly attitude of commander of the good ship George, in which the whole company embarked, and after a pleasant voyage, reached Plymouth on the twelfth of June, 1616. The bride was accompanied by a few of her kinsmen, among whom one of the most distinguished of them all suffered very soon after landing a most ludicrous discomfiture. He was one of the chief priests of his tribe and held in very high esteem by Powhatan, who had sent him for the special purpose of ascertaining by his own observation the number of ablebodied men about that strange tribe, the English might be able to oppose to his warriors. When Uttoniatoncakkin, the wise medicine-man, therefore left the ship to go on shore, he was seen to carry a white staff in his hand, and whenever he met a man on the wharves or in the streets of busy Plymouth, he made a notch in the stick. It was, of course, full in a short time, and the poor Indian utterly bewildered; he mentioned his mishap to his friends, who tried to explain the matter to him, but after his return to Virginia he could not help telling his master, the king, half reproachfully: "You sent me to number the English. Count the stars in heaven—count the sand on the sea-shore—then you will know the number of the English."

From Plymouth the young couple proceeded to London, and here the Indian princess, Lady Rebecca, as she was officially styled, received all the attention due to her rank. Her modest demeanor, and her interesting, attractive ways secured to her the affections of everybody, till the wise king, who was then seated on the throne of England actually became jealous and expressed a fear that poor Mr. Rolfe might presume upon his good luck in having married a royal princess! Absurd as the apprehension was, it showed that no doubt was entertained as to the social claims of Pocahontas, and that even by the monarch's morbidly historic mind she was regarded as a king's worthy daughter. We are told that she had previously already accustomed herself to civility, and now carried herself as the daughter of a king, so that there was no difficulty in the way when she appeared at Court under the patronage of Lady de la

War and was formally presented. Her debut was a perfect success, all doors were open to her, and rank and fashion vied with each other in doing honor to the strange maiden thus suddenly transplanted from savage life in distant forests to the strict etiquette and artificial manners of an English Court. We read glowing accounts of her being attended by divers persons of fashion and distinction, "while others of great rank and qualitiè have been very kind to her." Nor does she seem to have disliked the gay and brilliant life of London, for she appeared at the " Maskes" and other entertainments, and even at a great festival given with much state and pomp in her honor by the Bishop of London.

The close air, the dense fogs, and the oppressive smoke of the great city became, however, soon intolerable to one accustomed, as she was, to a life in the open air, and the beautiful, clear atmosphere of her native land. So she went down to Brentford, seven miles from London, the " City of Mud " of Thompson, where she lived for a few months in strict seclusion; and this was perhaps the happiest time of her whole life. No one came in contact with her who did not feel irresistibly attracted by the sweet and yet happy manner in which this child of Nature adapted herself to the strange life of the Old World, and her noble soul unfolded one beauty after another, as trials came and the end approached. The quaint chronicler of her life tells us in simple but touching words: "She had also by him a child, which she loved most dearly," but this blessing seemed to have filled the cup of her happiness to overflowing, for sonn after, in the month of March, 1617, she died at Gravesend, where she had hoped to embark for her native land, and there she was buried in the parish church. The building was unfortunately burned in 1727, but the parish-register was saved, and there we read the following entry: "1616. March 21. Rebecca Wrothe, wyffe of Thos. Wrothe, gent, a Virginia Lady borne, was buried in the channcell." It must be borne in mind that 1616 was then the civil year, while the historical year was 1617, and that the misspelling of the name presents no difficulties to those who remember that Shakespeare wrote his own name in a great variety of ways, that Sir Edward Coke's name was always spelt Cook by his own wife, and Sir Matthew Hale is printed as Hales in the Parliamentary journals. The clerk of the Vestry put down the name as it sounded in his ears, just as he would have written Chumley if he had been called upon to record the death of a Cholmondeley.

Thus ended the strange short life of this remarkable Indian maiden, and this is literally the only tangible relic of the last resting-place of "the first-fruit of the gospel in America."

Her husband, John Rolfe, leaving the infant in the hands of Sir Lewis Henkley at Plymouth, "who desired the care and education of him," returned to the Colony, where he was speedily appointed Recorder and Secretary. He appears repeatedly in the history of Virginia, now as the owner of four hundred acres, "planted in Rappahannock City, over against James City," and then again, is residing about two miles from the City of Henrico, where the Court-house afterwards stood, and the parsonage and glebe of New Varina were laid out. Tradition has it that the lands, which were for many generations called Pokahuntas, and formed at a later period one of the four towns of which Petersburg consisted, were originally given by Powhatan to John Rolfe as a marriage portion. The romance, however, does not extend beyond the life and the lineage of the Indian maid, for the widower married again and had other children, in whose behalf an application was made to a Virginia Court in 1622, by Henry Rolfe, brother to John Rolfe, and one of the adventurers who had come over two years before. John Rolfe himself died in 1622, unnoticed, and apparently unregretted.

The little infant, Pocahontas' child, had, in the meantime, a severe struggle for its life and future position. It had barely escaped a dangerous illness when misfortune and disgrace broke upon the house that had given him shelter, and threatened to involve him in one of the most tragic episodes of that eventful period. The distant kinsman, who had willingly assumed the responsible task of watching over the Indian king's grandchild, was a near connection and friend of Sir Walter Raleigh, and had, through his influence, and by the payment of a large sum of money, obtained the place of Vice-Admiral of Devon. To carry out his ambitious designs he earnestly coveted Raleigh's famous ship, which was then expected back from Guiana, and for this purpose engaged in one of the vilest conspiracies on record. Raleigh had fallen in disgrace, and Stukeley obtained, at his urgent request, the warrant for his arrest! He next engaged his noble and unsuspicious friend to accompany him on a journey to London, and at once the confidant and the executioner of the great statesman, he carried him to town, all friendship and devotion to his face, all villany and foul treachery in his heart. He even encouraged his victim in a plan of escape, carrying a warrant of indemnity for anything he might do for that purpose in his pocket, and rested not till he saw Raleigh safely in the tower and himself in possession of his ship. But revenge came in a way which probably no one had expected. Sir Walter declared on the scaffold and in sight of heavenly judgment, that he forgave Sir Lewis Stukeley, but felt bound in charity to caution all men against him and such as he was! The multitude mourned over Raleigh's fate and wept at his pathetic address, but they execrated the traitor, and Sir Lewis was henceforth known as Sir Judas. Raleigh's words had sealed his doom. He disappeared from society, but only to be dragged forth into broad daylight once more under an accusation of having clipped gold—the very guineas he had received from the Crown as the price of blood. To save himself, he first accused his own son; when this was of no avail, he bought his discharge with his last shilling, and then wandered about, homeless and friendless, till in August, 1620, Camden tells us, "Sir Lewis Stukeley, who betrayed Sir Walter Raleigh, died in a manner mad."

It was a happy escape for the poor Indian boy to be taken from the hands of such a man, though he enjoyed, no doubt, fewer advantages in the humble house of Henry Rolfe, his uncle, a modest citizen of London. When sufficiently strong to bear the fatigue of a long voyage, and after he had received a simple but sound education in England, he went to Virginia, settled down at Henrico, and became a person of fortune and some distinction in the colony. Every now and then he also appears in the early records of the Assembly and of local courts. Thus, in 1670, he sought and obtained leave from the General Assembly to visit his kinsman Opeehancanough, king of the Pamunkeys, and his aunt Cleopatre, his mother's sister. (Burk Va. II., p. 54.) Nothing is known of the pleasure he may have derived from this glimpse of Indian life; the drawbacks must have been serious. The king was the same grim old warrior whom Captain John Smith had detected in a vile plot to take his life, whereupon he had seized him boldly by a lock of his long hair, and, clapping a pistol to his heart, had led him out trembling before his people, thus saving his own life and that of his companions. Nor does his character seem to have improved as he grew older, for in a quaint pamphlet, " A Perfect Description of Virginia, London, 1649," we find him spoken of as " the bloody monster, upon a hundred years old." At another time Thomas Rolfe is the recipient of a special favor, an Act of the General Assembly, dated October, 1646, ordering: " That Leftenant Thomas Rolfe, shall have and enjoy for himselfe and his heires forever ffort James, alias Chickahominy Fort, with foure hundred acres adjoining the same." He had but one child, a daughter, who became the wife of Colonel Robert Bolling, and the mother of one son, Major John Bolling. The latter, however, left many children, "so that," says Stith, "this remnant of the Imperial family of Virginia, which long ran in a single person, is now increased and branched out in a very numerous progeny."

Long before him the remarkable man had also passed away with whom originated the whole strange drama. Captain John Smith had returned to London to end there a life unsurpassed in romantic adventure and noble achievements, in "mere oblivion." A contemporary writer says, with more feeling than skill:

> " If France or Spaine or any forren soile
> Could claime thee theirs—for these thy paines and toils
> Th'adst got reward and honor: now a days,
> What our own natives doe, we seldom praise."

The discoverer of New England and the founder of Virginia spent the closing years of his life in London unrewarded and unnoticed. The last scene of all, that ends this strange, eventful history, " is his burial in St. Sepulchres, Skinner street, and even there, in his last resting-place, ungrateful Fate seems to have pursued him, for the mural tablet that once recorded his name and his deeds, was destroyed in the great fire of London. All that reminds us now of him is a large flat stone in front of the communion-table, on which three Turks' heads—his arms —are still faintly visible, and thus our earliest romance, unsullied by crime and touching in its simplicity, ends, and

> " Like an insubstantial pageant faded
> Leaves not a rack behind.'

A FEW TOWN NAMES.

IV.

RECENT American author, impressed with the solemn duty of overcoming the natural bashfulness of his nation, and of making the outside world aware of a few points in which America might not be considered inferior to the Old World, wound up his essay with the words: "Physicians agree unanimously in admitting that man comes more readily into this world here than in any other part of the earth." It had long been known that the gates for going out of it were carefully kept wide open here at all times, and that a great variety of outlets were provided for leaving the world. But the news was cheering that the entrance doors also were many, and ready to swing open for the happy new-comer. The conclusion followed naturally, that a life so easily begun and so readily ended, could not well be presumed to be very slow in its course or very simple and solemn in its character. This was easily proved, for the American is a nomad: he travels from childhood up—now singly, and now in numbers. Railways and rivers, highways and

byways are incessantly thronged with a restless, surging crowd; mine inn is the home of thousands, and a "residence" in the stricter sense of the word is almost unknown. This system of perpetual motion naturally affects all around him; his States change their shape and size in times of peace as well as in war; his rivers wander hither and thither, and cities spring up over night, grow to a fair size, thrive and prosper, and as a new railway is opened or a new territory formed, they vanish over night to reappear at some distant place. Some of the oldest towns in the country have utterly disappeared, leaving no trace behind them; others rise suddenly like mushrooms and unfold their splendor in a few years, while still others content themselves with changing at least their name at short intervals, and often for no apparent reason. The great cities of Europe are known to us from time immemorial by their present designation, and in the rare cases where a double name is recorded one was intended for the great mass of the people and the other reserved for the small number of the initiated. Such, it is well known, was the case with Rome, which had its ancient sacred name of Valentia. In our New World, fortunately, the first stages in the history of great cities are still easily ascertained, and as many of the details will, no doubt, ere long be forgotten in the vast turmoil and reckless rush of our national life, it may not be amiss to record here some of the more striking instances.

In naming towns, as in our general nomenclature, it is very much to be regretted that Indian names have been either altogether ignored or at least sadly abused and disfigured by inattention. Hence there are but few important places in the Union which retain the original word in its purer form. Among these a prominent place is due to the one town which bears the national name of our mountains and rivers—Apalache. Oldmixon, not often reliable but generally well-informed, tells us that "the natives called the country *Apelchey* at first, from Norimbegua to Florida." (America I., p. 345.) The earliest mention made of the word occurs in an official report of Alonzo Enriquez, a Spanish officer who landed in April, 1527-8, on the coast of Florida, and was here informed by the Indians that there lay to the West a province called Apalache. How he could catch the sound is a mystery, as he tells us that this information came to him by signs; but the additional reports that "a quantity of metal," might be found there, evidently quickened his perception, for he really reached a village known by that name somewhere near the headwaters of the Savannah and Alatamaha Rivers. (Rel. Cabeça de Vaca. Valladolid, 1555.) In June, 1528, another adventurer of the same nation, Pamfilo de Narvaez, landed once more near the same place and again fell in with Apalache Indians, and, of course, again was allured by tempting stories of precious gold and silver to be found in some remote province—the fatal will-o'-the-wisp that led noble and ignoble spirits for ages into like ruin and destruction. Very nearly at the same time the "Mountains of Appalatey" are mentioned for the first time (Hakluyt III., p.

369), and thus there can be no doubt that the name is both ancient and widely spread over the continent. It is borne now by a modest but most interesting town in Florida, coupled with the Indian word *cola*, which is said to mean River, although Apalachicola is explained by one who is generally good authority as the town of low cottages on the river. (Purchas I., 744.) He accounts for the mention of low houses by the precaution taken to avoid the fatal effect of continual tempests, which prevail in those regions, but the explanation is doubtful.

When the unfortunate La Salle heard the sad news of the loss of his precious vessel, the Griffin, which he had built with his own hands near the Falls of Niagara, and which he hoped would bring him in a rich freight from Canada, the means of descending the great river of the West, his courage failed him and his heart was breaking. With the aid of a few faithful friends he built a little fort, surrounded by inaccessible swamps, which he called Crèvecoeur, and then set out to explore the country of the Illinois and to establish relations with the other great tribes. In the land of the Mascontins—the Wisconsins of later days—he struck a river which he heard called Chèkagon, and on its banks he found a village upon which he promptly bestowed that name. When on a later day, in the full flush of brilliant success, he took possession of the new country of Louisiana in the name of his sovereign, the King of France and Navarre, he for the first time wrote down in his *procès verbal* the name, of Chekagon, laying his claims " from the mouth of the

Mississippi to the waters of the Chekagon." (April 9 1682.) Father Membré tells us that the word meant Divine River, but in no Algonquin dialect can such an explanation be found. The name appears slightly modified in Jontel's Journal: " We arrived at Chicagou on the 29th of March, 1688," and here meant, not a river, but a fort, built, in all probability, on the very site of the great city of Chicago, rising just now phœnix-like from the ashes.

The town of Chillicothe, in the State of Ohio, is perhaps the only city in the United States which was once a considerable town of the Indians. Here the powerful nation of Shawnees, the Chats Sauvages or Wild Cats of the French, had so large a village that Daniel Boone, when brought as a captive to the place in 1778, saw a review of four hundred and fifty fully armed warriors, who were setting out for a forage upon the settlements of the whites. The question of the identity of this village with the present town, which bears that name, is, however, somewhat complicated by the fact that there were in those days at least three Chillicothes in existence. One spread its countless lodges over the beautiful Pickawa Plains, not far from the lovely site of the present city, and was famous as the place from which Logan sent his remarkable speech to Lord Dunmore, and is the same of which Boone gave so graphic an account. Another Chillicothe was on the Maumee, and a third on the Little Miami.

A town, small in size, but remarkable for its large

trade, bears the name of an extinct tribe of Indians, who seem to have been doubly unfortunate, as their own race was utterly destroyed, and even their ancient name survives only in a fragment. " Westward from Massachusetts Bay is situated a very spacious lake, called by the natives the Lake of Erocoise, which is far more excellent than the Lake of Genezareth in the country of Palestina," says Thomas Morton in his New England Canaan, printed in 1632. The name, although evidently intended for the French Iroquois, is here used to designate Lake Erie, of which Father Hennepin speaks as " Lake Erike, that is to say, the Lake of the Cat, as the Hurons call it." (Nouv. Découv., p. 77.) From this the transition is easy to " The Nation of the Eriez or the Cats," in Charlevoix, (Nouv. France I., p. 322,) and the name of Erie, given to the town and the great lake alike, is nowadays all that reminds us of the existence of a large and powerful nation, who were utterly destroyed by the Iroquois as early as the year 1654.

The town of Milwaukee awakens in the minds of those who take an interest in our early history the memory of two of those noble messengers of Christ who, though belonging to a hostile church, bore hearts as pure, as true and loving as any that ever beat under Puritan gown. They had left, like so many of their unselfish brethren, the pleasures and delights of fair France behind them, to plunge into the wilderness and to save the poor Indians. In the course of their wanderings westward, these two brave men, Allouez and Dablon, carrying no weapon but the cross, and having neither silver nor scrip for their journey, reached, at last, a dismal part of the land of the Miami's. They were nearly starved, but undaunted and undismayed, they preached day after day, till they came to a place which they heard the Indians call Mellioki, and which became a bright spot in their memories. They had a meal here ! " A little Indian corn, grinded small with little frogs gathered in a meadow." The opulent town of Milwaukee can fortunately receive missionaries more hospitably now, and reward them for the zeal and the privations of their predecessors.

In the heart of the State of New York, and in one of its fairest regions, there stands a small grove of venerable trees, hoary in their drapery of gray moss and strangely contrasting in their weird sadness with the smiling plain around them and the small busy town, the incessant hum of which is heard at a little distance. This is the spot where, in former days, powerful Indian nations met in solemn assembly and often formed plans which startled the hardy settler under the pines of Penobscot, struck alarm in the hearts of brave men to the far-off Mississippi, and even shook the mountain fastnesses of the distant Cherokees. Here the far-famed Six Nations kept their great council-fire burning forever ; here they assembled upon great and weighty occasions, and here the weal and woe of thousands were decided. The watch over the place and the care for the fire was entrusted to the Oneidas, who called themselves Onistaang, the people of the stone, from a sacred stone which followed them spontaneously and mysteriously wherever they went. Generation after generation passed away, and still they offered their yearly sacrifices on the magic altar, till their numbers had become too small for the sacred trust. Then, in our own day, Governor Seymour had the stone carried in solemn procession to the town of Utica (!), and there it was deposited in the beautiful cemetery, amid the low chants and grievous plaints of surviving Oneidas and Onondagas.

The town of Peoria recalls to us the often-forgotten fact that the Indians had their traditions, their pride of ancestry, and their long-cherished distinctions in quite as marked a manner as other nations. As they called the Delawares grandfathers, the Wyandots uncles, and the Mohicans elder brothers in acknowledgment of their varying antiquity, they bestowed similar names upon other tribes. Thus they spoke of the Florida Indians as of Seminoles or Runaways, because they were not an original tribe, but simply stray wanderers from other tribes, like the Upper Creeks and the Muscogees. Thus also, the name of Peouaria was given to a western tribe, from a word *piroue*, which means strange. For they lived a foreign community in the midst of the very sons of the soil, the Lenné-Lenapé, who were exceedingly proud of being the "men of all men," as their name signifies. This modest village of Indians, speaking a strange language, and hence so contemptuously called Foreigners, has since grown up into the beautiful city of Peoria on the lake of the same name.

Even more touchingly is the memory of early Indina life connected with the little town of Natick in Massachusetts; for the place owes its very existence and present form to the natives. Oldmixon tells us that "the Praying Indians combined together in a body and built a town by Charles River, in the midst of Massachusetts, to which they gave the name of Natick. It consists of three long streets, two on one side of the river and one on the other, with house-lots for every family." They formed here a church of their own, after the Presbyterian manner, and were prosperous and happy in 1660. It was here, also, that the great Apostle of the Indians had his famous "chamber in the wall," and the house is still shown to curious travellers, in an upper room of which a corner was partitioned off for the table and the bedstead of the pious Eliot, and where he wrote a large part of his immortal work.

The name of the forlorn town of Nantucket also is of Indian origin, Nantukes having been the primitive form, although it is occasionally traced back to a different source. When the different parts of the colony were distributed among the early settlers, the sandy-sterile island tempted no one; hence it was called Nan-tuck it, if we believe the mariners, who tell the story to the marines. The town has had more than its usual share of vicissitudes. At one time it was ceded to New York and straightway christened Sherburne: when it reverted to the parent colony it resumed its ancient name. Then it was almost entirely destroyed by fire, and in our own day it is nearly deserted, as the fisheries, which formerly supported and even enriched the inhabitants, have long ceased to be profitable. Fortunately it has quite a number of descendants, thanks to the fact that her bold, indefatigable sailors are well-known in nearly every part of the globe. Thus San Francisco has its suburb near the port called New Nantucket, and a faraway island in the Pacific even bears the name of Nantucket, the sponsors in all these cases coming from the original town "Down East."

It was probably one of the proudest days in the great De Soto's life when he approached, on the 18th October, 1570, the large Indian city, of which such wonders had been foretold, and where his excited imagination already saw all the treasures of a vast kingdom placed at his disposal. He was riding in the haughty consciousness of his power, at the head of the largest force of European soldiers which our part of the New World had yet seen, and by his side the gigantic Black Warrior, Tuscaloosa, the noble chief of the people whose capital he was approaching. A vast crowd of men and women covered the beautiful plain as far as eye could see, and the heights overhanging the Alabama River also were thronged with a wondering multitude. The great explorer felt his heart swell with delight as the large, well-built town, with its countless houses and stately temples, fell upon his eye; he did not heed, in his triumph, the dark clouds that hung on every countenance and the fierce, defiant fire that flashed from the eyes of the warriors. Alas! before he could renew his mournful march to the Mississippi, the whole of that magnificent town was to be laid in ashes, more than half of his faithful followers were to be buried on its site, and over six thousand Indian warriors were to fall in defence of their country. For Maubila, as he heard the town called, was one of the few large, fortified cities of which we have any record in the annals of Indian history, and the Maubilians the bravest people ever encountered by the Spaniards. They were conquered by De Soto, thanks to his horses, his firearms and the indomitable courage of his brave men; but he paid dearly for the victory, and when he left the ill-fated spot, he had lost the flower of his army, the whole of his personal property, ammunition and armor included; and, most grievous loss of all, the bouyant hopes and haughty confidence that had kept his courage up amid so many trials and vexatious delays. From that day the name of Mavilla, as the Spaniards preferred to write it, became a household word with all the adventurers who thronged our harbors and garrisoned our forts, but it was transferred from the old Indian town on what is now called Choctaw Bluff, to the mouth of the river Maubile, as the name appears in the reports of early French settlers. Marigny de Mandiville, a brave Protestant soldier, here built in June, 1722, a strong fort, which he named after the great Condé—the cornerstone, with the date of the first attempt made in 1717, having been found by our own troops some years after the fort, rechristened by the British as Fort Charlotte, had been taken from the latter. How little stability there was for generations in these

Indian names of our towns, may be seen from the fact that James Glen, from 1739 to 1755, the able Governor of South Carolina, in his report to the Duke of Argyll, speaks of a " River Moville, falling into the Bay of Mexico."

Another southern town began its existence where other places generally end it—in ruins. This is the city of Yazoo, the first settlers of which thoughtlessly adopted for their new home the name which they had heard applied to the place by the surrounding Indians, the Choctaws and Chickasaws. They were not aware that the vast number of mounds and ruined fortifications which are strewn along the course of the Yazoo River, and in which those tribes beheld the last traces of the works of the former owners of the soil, had led them to bestow upon the stream and the whole district the name of Yazoo—the Ruins. A still stranger mistake was made by Major James T. Savage, the discoverer of the far-famed Yosemité Valley, on Merced River, on the western slope of the Sierra Nevada. Pursuing, with a mere handful of men, a band of predatory Indians, he came suddenly in sight of the magnificent spectacle, which has not its equal upon earth, and having just learned the word Yosemité, which he then thought to be the Indian name of the Grizzly Bear, the emblem of California and the most remarkable inhabitant of those regions, he very naturally gave that name to the Valley. One of the most striking features of this world of wonders, fortunately, bears a more appropriate name. This is the Sequoia gigantea, the colossal pine tree, which, now singly and now in groups, adorns the great valley; it is so named in honor of Sequoia, the famous Cherokee Indian who invented, by his genius, an alphabet for his tribe, and enjoys the unique honor of conferring an Indian's name upon a recent discovery in science.

In spite of all the violent changes to which these Indian names of towns have been subjected, and in spite of the frequent blunders of which they remain permanent witnesses, they seem to be far preferable to the majority of English names, which were either transferred from other uses to towns or specially made for the purpose. The subject of our town-names of this class is an inexhaustible source of ridicule and cheap wit for foreign critics, and yet even the genius of a Dickens did not succeed in coining a new name for his type of a Western city, but had to content itself with copying from the Westover MSS. the happy name of Eden. That is, of course, no reason why the proud American should boastfully have twenty-four Edens in the Union, besides six earthly New Jerusalems. He does not much believe in ancient myths, and hence contradicting the poet's assertion that, *Ilium fuit*, he has sixteen Troys. The subject of classic names, however, is a peculiarly painful one, thanks to the preference given to this class by one of the early Surveyor-Generals of the State of New York, De Witt, who is responsible for the Uticas and Ithacas, the Homers and Virgils, the Romes and Athens, which abound in the Empire State, and from thence spread all over the Union.

Why Demosthenes should be alone forgotten of all the great classic authors, is hard to tell; but even Shakespeare is badly treated; he has but one town named after him in Arkansas, and the two cities of Romeo and Juliet are but a sorry consolation. There is no objection to be made to well-meaning settlers who determine to identify their new homes with Enterprise or Energy, with Friendship or Harmony, Energy or Equality; but why they should ever choose Embarrassment is wholly unintelligible. Nor is it easy to understand the taste of the nine communities who chose to recognize and honor Cain by assuming his name, while not one has done the same honor to Abel.

The mere absurdity of names being thus promiscuously and arbitrarily bestowed upon towns and cities is bad enough. No traveller in the State of New York can well repress a feeling of impatience, when, after leaving Carthage in the morning, he is made to dine at Leyden, and sups, if so inclined, at Denmark, or if he should choose another route, reaches Russia by noon and Norway before night. Nothing but darkest ignorance or grossest indifference can excuse such a proceeding, although indolence has gone even farther and bodily transferred a whole county from the State of New York to that of Wisconsin, every name of town, village and hamlet, being faithfully reproduced. But it is not easy to imagine that this is all of the evil. It cannot be but that some influence is exercised by the name of a place over its inhabitants. It need not be the somewhat painful effect which Piousville has on its citizens, who are open to the suspicion of being pious villains ; but how can the man who lives in Dirttown (Ga.), Robtown (Va.), Gin-Henry (Mo.), or Smallpox (Ill.), preserve his self-respect through life ? Can a man confess that he lives at Longacoming, Fuddletown or Bugaboo, and expect to be looked upon like any other respectable gentleman? Kickaboo, Wegee or Maxinkuckee would seem to be infinitely preferable names, though startling enough at first sight. There is a class of men among us who can perhaps best afford to connect themselves with such names : it is those who themselves enjoy peculiar designations, like Mr. Undone Boots, of Albany, and Mr. Unfledged Hawk, of New York, to say nothing of men of historic renown, like Mr. Preserved Fish. With such an endless variety of names at our disposal, and enjoying, besides, according to a most learned opinion delivered in the courts of New York, the unlimited right of " assuming a name at will," it is a wonder that so few new forms appear in our geographies and directories. When new territories are to be named and new towns to be christened, nothing but repetition is thought of, and hence the multitude of counties and post-towns which have the same designation. The same poverty of invention appears in christening children, and apparently the fatality extends even to the increased facility of changing names by means of divorce. Quite recently a case in point appeared in the Court of Indianapolis. An enterprising woman, desirous of making a new experiment in matrimony, complained that she had been married five times already, without ever succeeding in obtaining a new "start." Born a Smith, she had first married a Smith, then a German Schmidt, next an English Smythe, after him a Smithe, and now she appeared on record as Mrs. Smythe once more. The judge was inexorable, and she may have to end as she began— a Smith forever. A Western town had a still more grievous trial to undergo. The first settlers had called the place Grasshopper Falls, a name which the good town considered unpleasantly suggestive of a peculiarity of Kansas, and therefore applied in 1863 to the Legislature for leave to change. A wag had suggested Sauterelle, the French name of the destructive insect, and Sauterelle the lawgivers decreed it should be hereafter. The common people, however, unable to repeat the foreign sound, in a little while transformed it into Sowtail, and so great was the distress of certain inhabitants of the place at receiving letters addressed to them at Sowtail, that they penitently returned to the Grasshopper of their early days.

This tendency to corrupt or Anglicise French names is a fertile source of odd and apparently inexplicable names in our country. Wherever the French first settled and gave names to local features, the same ludicrous process of utter transformation has taken place; mountains, rivers and towns, have all fared alike. The Bay of Fundy has a marked feature in a tall mountain, which is almost constantly overhung with huge masses of cloud, and was, hence, called by the early missionaries Chapeau Dieu (God's Hat); it is now Shepody Mountain. At the other end of the Northern Continent lies the Bay, once known as Anse des Cousins (Mosquito Bay); sailors and settlers alike now speak of it only as Nancy Cousin's Bay. A beautiful river in St. Lawrence County, New York, flowing through fertile lands and enriching the soil by periodical overflows, was called La Grasse Rivière (the Fertile River), by the French Canadians, who lived at the mouth, near the head of St. Regis Island. Falling into English hands it was promptly naturalized as Grass River. A sadder fate was that of the low, dismal stream on which the town of Galena is situated. When first discovered in 1700 by Le Seuer, it obtained the name of La Rivière des Fèves (Bean River), from the immense masses of wild beans which were found growing on its banks. The beans disappeared when the country was settled, and with them the meaning of the name; but as the river had in the meantime established an unenviable notoriety for "fever and ague," it was naturally transformed into La Rivière de la Fièvre (Fever River), and such it remained till in the year 1854 the Legislature of Illinois, by a special Act, ordered it to be called Galena River. That State, early explored by French missionaries and rich in French names, abounds hence also in curious corruptions of this kind. Thus the Marais d'Ogée has become Meredosia; an ill-reputed creek, known as Mauvaise Terre, is now Movistar Creek; an out-of-the-way passage, Chenal Ecarté, rejoices in the euphonious name of Snicarty; Aukas is now Okau, and Bon Pas Prairie has degenerated into Bompare, and will probably end, like Bon Père, in a vulgar Bumper. The farther West we go the more striking become these corruptions. A cape on the Upper Mississippi, called by the early French voyagers Cap à l'ail, Garlic Cape, is now known as Capolite; Lewis and Clark found two rivers Thieraton already in their day changed into Charaton; la Rivière qui court, had become Quicurre River; and a branch of the Red River of Lake Winnipeg, originally called Rivière Cheyenne, "from the Cheyenne Indians living on its borders," had gradually changed into Rivière Chien, and was then translated into Dog River! Towns which received their names in course of a regular process seem to have been by no means more fortunate, thanks to unfortunate accidents or the very pardonable ignorance of first settlers. Such was the fate of a Connecticut town, which was once a simple farmstead, owned by a plain man of strong religious feelings. His zeal steadily outran his knowledge, and his Scripture quotations were frequent but not always correct. At a town-meeting he referred to the words of the prophet Isaiah: "Who is this that cometh from Eden, with dyed garments from Bozrah?" and took it into his head that Bozrah was a prophet. He was laughed at, and consequently became prouder than ever of the many sayings of the Prophet Bozrah. Soon he himself was known by no other name, his homestead was called so, and when in later years it grew up into a considerable town, it still remained Bozrah. The same State once deprived a town by a clerical blunder of its beautiful name. An Indian village, called Hammonasset, was settled in 1665 by whites, and in remembrance of their distant home named Kenilworth. When, however, the Assembly of Connecticut, in 1705, issued a regular patent for its incorporation, the copying clerk wrote it Killingworth, and such it has continued to this day.

The Queen City escaped only by chance a similar grievous fate. Among the first settlers on the beautiful river there were a few shrewd men who had carefully noted the fact that the treacherous stream, in all its frequent and violent overflowings, never rose to the height of certain bluffs, which were seen nearly opposite the mouth of a small stream, Licking River. Under the leadership of an old schoolmaster, John Filson, they clubbed their scanty means together and bought these highlands ; then a meeting was held to christen the new purchase. After much wrangling the knotty question was referred to the learned man among them, and he made good use of the occasion to air his learning. After considerable study and meditation he produced the beautiful name of Losantiville, which was accepted by acclamation ; it sounded so grand, and when he deigned to explain it, the meaning was so very clear and striking ! Was not *L* a reminder of L, the first letter of Licking River, and did not *os* mean in Latin, mouth? So here was the mouth of Licking River. And did not *anti* mean over against, while *ville*, everybody knew, was the genteel name for a town. Here was the whole geography of the new city in a nutshell ! The people around, in their envy, no doubt, dubbed it Mosaic Town ; and jealous writers point out, with a sly hint at poetical justice, that the unlucky schoolmaster was, a short month afterwards, murdered on the Miami River by a single Indian. It is well known how, by the good taste of General St. Clair, then Governor of the Territory, the city was rescued from that hideous name, to be called " Cincinnata, in honor of the order of the Cincinnati, and to denote the chief place of their residence."

The cases in which town names serve to recall the great names of our early history are unfortunately but few in number. One of the most remarkable of this class is probably the town of Duluth, which has not only suddenly sprung into existence, but, as by the touch of a magic wand, acquired an importance great enough to make its name instantly known all over the country. The offspring of yesterday, it nevertheless carries us back to the year 1680, when, we are told by Father Hennepin, " the Sieur du Luth was arrived there from Canada " (Nouv. Découv. p 245). That energetic soldier, a man of great talent and indefatigable zeal for the missions among the Indians, had been promoted from a simple captain of marines to the command of the outlying posts, which at a later period dotted the whole long line of communication from the St. Lawrence to the Gulf of Mexico. In the last year of Frontenac's administration, Du Luth was sent to the far West to open new sources of traffic among the numerous Indian tribes on Lake Superior, and in 1728 built the fort, which bore his name. By the side of such appropriate designations it appears a matter of all the greater regret to find the natural suggestions wilfully neglected, and old names applied to new and insignificant places. Thus there is in the heart of the State of New York a spot apparently marked out by nature and by history alike to become a memorial of the days of the Indians. A vast mound rises from a smiling plain, and overhangs, as usually, the banks of a beautiful stream; the enormous earth ramparts, which formerly surrounded it, are still distinctly traceable, although now overgrown with noble forest trees, and all speaks eloquently of the great centre of Indian life, that once, no doubt, was dear to many a proud tribe. On the summit of the hill there rises in mournful loneliness a single obelisk, with the plaintive words rudely carved on its western side: "Who is there to mourn for Logan?" recalling forcibly the touching words of the bereaved warrior. The whites had slain every kinsman of their old ally and friend, so that he could justly say: There runs not a drop of my blood in the veins of any living creature! But Indian mounds and Indian bravery all were set aside in favor of a weakly sentimentality, which preferred the poet's fiction and called the city Auburn. Inattractive as the name of Circleville is, we prefer it as suggestive of a remarkable memorial of early Indian life. The town, lying twenty-six miles south of Columbus, in the State of Ohio, is built within a vast circumvallation, raised in most ancient times by the Indians on the banks of the Scioto. The site is an accurate circle, encompassing nearly forty-four acres, and by its side rises an equally accurate square, containing the same amount of land, and although both circle and square have been surveyed by well-trained engineers, no error has yet been detected!

Very different memories are recalled by the name of another town on the Belle Rivière of the French, in the same State—Gallipolis. In the year 1788 Joel Barlow, well known as one of the earliest American poets and a diplomatist of no small notoriety, was authorized to go to Europe for the purpose of encouraging and directing immigration to this country. He filled France with stirring appeals and flaming advertisements; the lands of Ohio were praised as a very paradise upon earth, which produced wheat and maize without labor, while the trees of the forest gave sugar, and the shrubs all around furnished candles. The poor down-trodden French hailed eagerly the news of this promised land, where taxes were unknown, bread was abundant, and the climate the same as their own. Soon five hundred emigrants sailed for the Eldorado; but they had hardly landed on our shores when their troubles commenced. They were unprepared for the long journey from the seaports to the banks of the Scioto, and when, after infinite delays and much cruel suffering, they were at last enabled to behold the land "where milk and honey flowed," the disappointment was grievous. The fertile fields were covered with dense forests, that had to be cleared before any crop could be raised; the maple trees refused to yield sugar save in mid-winter, and the myrtle-bushes, that were to produce wax, were few in number and difficult of access. Then came the same trouble which so frequently endangered the existence of Virginia in her earliest days: the abundance of gentlemen and cunning artisans among the emigrants, and the absence of useful men, inured to hard work and familiar with husbandry. Artists, peruke makers and skilled laborers abounded, but although there is on record a well-authenticated story of a French dancing-master, who accumulated a fortune by teaching a Southern Indian tribe, the Creeks, the graces of minuets and contre-dances, the natives of Ohio were not equally appreciative. A still greater misfortune occurred and filled the measure of their misery: the Scioto Company, under whose auspices they had come out, failed to pay for the lands, which reverted to the United States Government, and thus the poor helpless new-comers were left to shift for themselves, unable to converse with their neighbors, without money and without experience. It is hard to understand how they could summon courage, under such distressing circumstances, to mark out the boundaries of their new settlement, which was by the Company dubbed in their honor Gallispolis, a horrible compound and a wretched substitute for the simpler Frenchtown of other States. It was here that Volney saw them in 1796, and was filled with compassion for their miserable fate. Government had the year before " donated " to the poor refugees 20,000 acres of good land at Sandy Creek, which, with an additional grant of 1,200 acres, made a few years later, gave the name of French Grant to that region. But the defeat of General St. Clair on the Miamis, in 1791, had laid the country open to Indian assaults, and here were the unlucky Frenchmen living in huts and caves, suffering from miasmas, frost and snow, and decimated by the tomahawk of the red men. Many a sad year passed away, and hundreds of the poor immigrants were buried by the river-side, before the town recovered from its early trials and rose to become what it now is, one of the most flourishing cities of a great State.

There are, of course, Salems innumerable in the Union; from the first permanent town in Massachusetts, so called on 24th June, 1629, to the last "city" in Utah, for Puritans and Moravians, Catholics and Protestants, all united in their veneration of the blissful name of Peace, and loved to bestow it upon the safe harbors in which they hoped to find the repose denied them in the old country. But there is only one Jerusalem in this country which claims to be like David's town, the birth-place of a new faith. This is a small town in the State of New York, lying in the midst of wild and romantic scenery, although surrounded, in former days, by a belt of desert and wilderness. A fair Quakeress—whether purposely deceiving others or self-deceived, who can tell?—came to this remote and almost unknown spot in the early part of this century and chose it as the home of her friends and followers, who called themselves The Universal Friends. By her matchless beauty, her native shrewdness and truly amazing tact, she succeeded in gathering around her a number of wealthy, well-meaning adherents, who built themselves humble log cabins, while they housed their idol in a magnificent mansion. Here she lived and ruled for years, claiming that since the day of her miraculous recovery from a dangerous illness, the power and spirit of Christ dwelt in her and enabled her to do wonders on earth and to secure to her faithful followers an entrance into heaven. She is said to have been the first inventor of the costume that became afterward known as the Bloomer, and to have enforced its use, together with celibacy and temperance. Nor did the charm which she had woven around the hearts of her devoted followers cease with her death, in 1829; another crafty woman, Rachel Malon, took up the deception, and maintained the new faith and the quaint worship for some time afterwards. Then the frail structure broke down and the town fell back into the number of unmeaning and unknown Jerusalems, of which there are but too many in this country.

A far more pleasing sound is the name of Providence, which Oldmixon curiously enough prefers calling Prudence. (America I, p. 65). We all know how obstinate but conscientious Roger Williams was led, by the suggestions of Governor Winthrop, to leave Massachusetts Colony and seek a new home beyond her oppressive jurisdiction; how he crossed on a bitter cold January day, 1636, with only five companions, the river Seekonk, and landed near a spring at the first inhabited nook of the future State of Rhode Island. He purchased, before he broke ground, the land from the now extinct tribe of Narragansett Indians, and in 1674, in commemoration of God's providence to him in his distress, he called the place

Providence, and thus laid the foundations of a new commonwealth, destined to become one of the brightest stars in the galaxy of the Union. His boundless charity led him to receive with open arms whosoever came, for he said: "I desire it might be for a shelter for persons distressed for conscience." He had of course to pay the penalty incurred everywhere and in all ages by such unlimited toleration, and his beloved town fared badly, for a time, in public estimation. The Rev. Cotton Mather did not hesitate to call the first settlers a generation of Libertines, Familists, Antinomians, whose posterity, for want of schools of learning and a public ministry, are become so barbarous as not to be capable of speaking either good English or good sense" (Oldmixon, America, p. 204). W. C. Bryant has in one of his poems revived the name of Rogue's Island, which Connecticut malice, long ago, applied to parts of the new State, "because their neighbours on the East were so peculiar." The good people who followed Roger Williams were, however, made of too stern stuff to mind such slanders, and already, in 1642, a body of Puritans, driven out from New England on account of their "peculiar" views, went to Virginia and built near the present site of Annapolis, in Maryland, a New-Providence, for which they secured from the Legislature a special Act (April 9, 1649), securing to them perfect liberty of conscience.

Nor is this the only example of a town name going on its travels and reappearing in various parts of the Union. Dorchester, for instance, might be called a migratory town, without doing it injustice. The ancestor is, of course, old Dorchester in England, dating back from the days of the Romans ; from thence the Rev. John White sent out, in 1630, a colony of independent churchmen, who founded a new Dorchester on a neck of land at Mattapan, in Massachusetts. Although the colony throve and prospered, discontent soon broke out among the settlers, and a considerable number formed themselves into an independent church, with their minister and deacons, for the purpose of moving in a body to South Carolina. They declared it to be their duty " to encourage the settlement of churches and the promotion of religion in the Southern plantations "—a tender regard for the consciences of others which has not become extinct since those days. Thus there arose a third Dorchester, in the South, where, on the 2d February, 1696, the Lord's Supper was for the first time administered, and the settlement nobly inaugurated. The town—on a branch of Ashleigh River—prospered handsomely and soon became quite famous by having within its precincts the first free school ever known in the province, which was formally established, in 1724, by a special Act of Assembly. The tract of land, however, which they had purchased, proved too small, and could not be extended, as it was surrounded by fever-breeding marshes. The entire population, the town of Dorchester in fact, went forth, therefore, to Georgia, where they obtained from the Governor of the Colony an ample grant of land to the south of the Oguebee River, at a place called Midway. Here, still another Dorchester was founded, and to good purpose, for the colonists seem not only to have maintained their character, but bequeathed it unblemished and undiminished to their children. A succession of excellent and truly pious ministers preserved their religious principles with remarkable fidelity for many generations, while their independent spirit appears to have grown even stronger in adversity. For these good people of Dorchester actually sent delegates of their own to the Continental Congress long before the Colony of Georgia had taken measures to promote the common cause, and it was in grateful acknowledgment of this zeal that St. John's County, in which they lived, was subsequently by special legislative action re-christened Liberty County.

There is a curious contrast between the martial sound of the old Indian name, Musketicook, or Musketaquick, which once belonged to an ancient town of Massachusetts, and its more recent name of Concord. The former has, of course, nothing to do with murderous muskets, but simply means Dead Stream, in allusion to the sluggish nature of the river, that was so called, and Concord bears its sweet name, not inappropriately, in memory of the peaceful and righteous measures by which the first settlers, in 1635, obtained the consent of the aborigines to colonise on their land. Norwalk, in Connecticut, shows on the contrary the absurd manner in which our early towns were occasionally named. Here also the lands were legitimately acquired from the Indians by purchase, in 1641, but so far from perpetuating the memory of an important transaction in the name of the new settlement, they only thought of recalling the irrelevant fact that it was "one day's walk North into the country"! How much more touching is the manner in which Paris, in New York, received its peculiar name! It lies in a part of the State which is already rich in unfortunate cities, bearing the names of all the great towns of the Old World, and Paris, therefore, is also constantly suspected of being but one of the numerous brood of Londons and Romes, Syracuses and Smyrnas. It owes its name, however, to a very different source. In the year 1789 a great scarcity prevailed in that whole district, and here and there starvation was actually impending. The small settlement in Oneida County, only a few months old, suffered especially, and all hearts were heavy and sad. But help was at hand ; a well-to-do miller and merchant at Fort Plain, on the Mohawk, heard of the distress, and immediately dispatched whole wagon-loads of "Virginia Corn," which he distributed among the sufferers, requiring no payment, but giving them ample credit. By his liberality they were saved from imminent danger, and as an expression of their gratitude, petitioned the Legislature soon after to bestow the name of their benefactor, Isaac Paris, upon the town, which owed to him its existence.

Towns which received their names in honor of some reigning monarch, some powerful nobleman, or illustrious commoner in Europe, are, of course, very numerous throughout the country, and represent every class of society, from the sovereign on his throne to the demagogue who sent him to exile. Nor are English sponsors alone responsible for our town names. There is Marietta, on the beautiful river called by the Indians the Elk Eye, but known to us as Muskingum, which marked by its foundation the first day of the existence of the State of Ohio. A small number of persons from New England had bought of the Ohio Land Company a superb tract of rich bottom lands on the river, and on the 2d of July, 1788, met there in solemn assembly to name their future city. A greater confusion of names was probably never seen united within so small a place. The town they agreed to call Marietta, in honor of poor Marie Antoinette, whose fate just then excited universal sympathy in all feeling hearts; the first chosen officer of the new community was Mr. Return Jonathan Meigs; the square on which a blockhouse was erected for protection against the Indians had the name of Campus Martius conferred upon it, and the great road through the covered way was modestly called Sacra Via. Far off, near the sea-coast, another town had long ago been built to perpetuate the memory of a queen, whose end was less tragic, perhaps, but by no means less melancholy. Here, in a long-forgotten colony, loyal Swedes had raised a fort which they called, "after the little jasmine bud in the royal conservatory," Fort Christina, for the martyr-king's infant daughter was then seated upon the throne of Sweden. It is not a little curious that as her prestige waned and she gradually lost one noble quality after another, till at last she forsook even her faith and died in distress at Rome, the distant colony also declined, and after a short though peaceful career, ended in utter destruction. In America also the place that once knew the unfortunate queen knows her no more, and when an accident recalls her memory, the wonder is great. Thus men marvelled when, upon building a new fort on the old site, a small silver coin was found on the spot, with the arms of the house of Vasa on one side, and on the other the inscription, " Christina D. G. Re. Sve. 1633." It was only when on the reverse were read the words : *Moneta Novi Regni Suec,* Coin of the Kingdom of New Sweden, that the Christina of the face was recognized as " By the Grace of God Queen of Sweden."

The stately name of St. Augustine conjures up before our mind's eye the brave company of Spaniards, who, on September 2d, 1562, under their gallant leader Menendez, sailed up the beautiful bay, which was then first seen by Europeans, and bestowed upon it the name of one of the most eloquent sons of Africa, and at the same time one of the most venerated fathers of the Church, whose day it was in the calendar. What a brilliant pageant it must have been, when the great captain landed at the head of an army of a thousand men, with banners flying, trumpets sounding, and heavy guns thundering for the first time over the glorious, peaceful landscape ! Before him walked the priest with the symbol of his faith borne by an anolyte, and amid solemn ceremonies and imposing displays, the sacred name was bestowed upon the future city. Thus were the foundations laid of the town, which is by forty years the oldest in the Union, and which actually dates back to a time when no Englishman of any sect had yet set foot on the soil of America, long before the pilgrims landed at Plymouth, or Captain John Smith sailed up the King's River. But it is sad to think how soon the blooming fields of the infant town were to be baptized in blood! For only a few days later Jean Ribault entered the same waters, and was followed a year later by Laudonnière with his Protestant soldiers, and forthwith broke out the fierce, passionate warfare that had already deluged the Old World, cursing the New World also with its terrible deeds of violence. Ere the year had come to a close, the blood of six hundred brave Protestant Frenchmen had been poured out like water upon the virgin soil, and the boastful declaration of the victorious Spaniards, that they had slain them "not as Frenchmen but as heretics," proclaimed to the amazed world that Abel's murder bore its bloody seed in America also. To this day the horror of the massacre seems to cling to the spot, and while the traveller looks with wonder at houses in St. Augustine bearing the date of 1571 as the year of their erection, he shudders with awe as he beholds the subterranean cells in which but a few years ago workmen found long iron boxes standing upright, each of which contained a human skeleton in irons. In noble contrast with the terrible christening of the old town of St. Augustine stands the manner in which the Golden City on the Pacific obtained its saintly name. Here, in the year of our nation's birth, a band of devoted Spanish monks, full of holy zeal and willing self-denial, founded a modest station to proclaim the glad tidings of "peace upon earth and good-will among men " to the Indians of that region. The old " Mission, " built of adobe bricks, still stands, lonely and deserted, about three miles south of the stately City Hall, which crowns the great city, to which the Franciscan brethren bequeathed the name of their patron saint, San Francisco de Assisi.

A few of our town names are suggestive of great historical associations, which, like other events of the kind, seem likely to be soon entirely effaced from the memory of coming generations. Thus there nestles in the Western part of Old Virginia a modest little town in the mountains which bears a name that once graced an Empire. The great Lord Botetourt had in England a country-seat called Fin Castle, and this name he bestowed in 1774 upon a part of a county, which already was known by his own name as Botetourt County. The region was inhabited by a mere handful of settlers, and the county-seat, the ancestor of the present town of Fincastle, consisted of little more than a few humble log cabins. But the County, thanks to the ignorance which in those days still prevailed as to all the territory lying west of the Alleghany Mountains, was described in the Act of Assembly, that gave it a legal existence, as " extending to the Mississippi ! " And so it did, for only two years later a slice was taken from it to make the great State of Kentucky, while the remainder was cut up into more counties, the town alone retaining its name of Fincastle. Another offspring of the little village was Fort Fincastle, to which it gave its name about the same time, when it was deemed important to protect the western part of the country, on the Ohio, by a considerable stronghold against Indians and Frenchmen. The fort, when refitted a few years later, was re-christened Fort Henry, in honor of the great Patrick Henry, then Governor of Virginia, and finally grew up into the city of Wheeling.

Very different interests are connected with some of the twin-names in which not a few of our towns rejoice. Thus Saybrook, in the State of Connecticut, perpetuates the united memory of Viscount Say and Seale and of Lord Brook. The former had purchased of the unfortunate Pequods, in 1634, a portion of their territory in order to carry out the purposes of a grant which the Earl of Warwick had assigned to John Pym, John Hampden and other famous Puritans of his day, who wanted a place of retreat from the persecutions with which they were threatened. Lord Brook, one of the staunchest puritans in England, had not, like Lord Say and Seale, come over himself, but sent his agent, George Fenwick, to purchase lands and lay out a town at the mouth of Connecticut river. Wilkesbarre, in Pennsylvania, on the contrary, bears the joint names of the great agitator John Wilkes and Colonel Barré, in grateful acknowledgment of their advocacy of the American cause during the struggle of the revolution. Perth Amboy, a town of New Jersey, on the other hand, seems to show by the unwillingness of the two names to combine into one, the different origin of the two elements: the former being taken from James, Earl of Perth, one of the two proprietors of East Jersey, the latter a corruption of the original name of Ompage, by which the Indians designated the place, and which occurs quite frequently yet in the early records of New Jersey. Thus it is called even in the works of Richard Barclay, whom Oldmixon calls " the famous " Scotch Quaker, who wrote a defence of Quakerism in better Latin than any of his answerers could boast.

There are scattered all over the Eastern states a large number of towns which startle the visitor from foreign shores at first sight by their peculiar biblical character. With a few exceptions, such as Ephrata in Pennsylvania, these places belong all to that remarkable brotherhood of excellent pious men who are among us generally known as Moravians, while their legal title is the *Unitas Fratrum*, the United Brethren, bestowed upon them by Great Britain in 1737. Moravia, on the Owasco Flats, in the State of New York, bears still the name of the original home of the brethren, who came mostly from Moravia and Bohemia, and had formerly one of the most successful Indian schools of the North; its namesake in distant Kansas is, on the other hand, among the youngest of such settlements. For their eminently practical and simple plan is to go wherever there seems to be a need for the preaching of the gospel, and as their devoted sons and daughters used to accept the helpmate intended for them by the divine will, as the lot, reverently cast amid invocations of the Deity, decided for them, so they obeyed the same self-chosen voice as to their future destination in any part of the globe. Thus they once showed strikingly their true character as a United Brotherhood, embracing all the children of men without distinction, when a number of their followers arrived in May, 1749, in the city of New York. They brought with them two intelligent natives of Greenland, who had been converted and consecrated as ministers of their faith, and were met there by a deputation of brethren from Philadelphia, containing two of our own Indians and two natives of Surinam, who had in like manner been brought under the influence of the gospel, and gladly joined hands with the new-comers. Occasionally their settlements in the New World were named so as to recall special memories of the Old World, as when Wachoria, a lordly domain of 100,000 acres in North Carolina, was so called after the Vale of Wachau, formed by a river in Austria, the Vir Wash, and owned by the ancestors of the great Count Zinzendorf, whose benevolent acts and signal services are gratefully remembered in this country as well as in Europe. Lites, in Pennsylvania, leads us still farther back, for it bears the name of a domain in Bohemia, where George Podiebrad, Regent of the kingdom, established the very first congregation of the United Brotherhood to serve God in quietness and peace, in contrast with the fierce and relentless proceedings of their more violent brethren, the Tabontes. This is one of the few Slavic names which we have preserved in our country, and recalls the ancient date of 1457, which some of the brethren look upon as the year of the foundation of their church.

The precise date when the first Moravians reached

this country has not yet been absolutely settled, but their first permanent station was in all probability an Indian school, established in 1735, at Ebenezer, on an island in the Savannah river, about an hour's sail above the city, to which the "king of the Creeks came to hear the good word." They were not allowed long to live in peace here, for upon a war breaking out with Georgia's implacable enemies, the Spaniards, they were summoned to take up arms and assist in the defence. As this was against their principles, they preferred to abandon their new homes, their worldly goods and all their bright hopes, and moved in a body to Pennsylvania, then the asylum of all persecuted men, and here, on a branch of the Delaware, which they called the Lecha, but which has since been Anglicised into Lehigh, they attempted once more a mission among the Indians. The principal settlement was to be called Beth-lechem, the House on the Lehigh, but Count Zinzendorf, who was then travelling through this country in behalf of the Brotherhood, changed the name. He had reached the place a day or two before Christmas (1741), and celebrating the great festival in the roomy stable of the only cabin which then marked the site of the town, he improvised, during the watches of Christmas Eve, a hymn, beginning with the words : "Not Jesus, no Bethlehem !" This line, the place and the date of its composition, led to the name of Bethlehem being chosen for the new mission, which soon grew in size and importance and is now one of the chief places of the Moravians. Almost all the early names of their subsequent settlements were given by Zinzendorf, either in person or by letter; some merely from choice, as Bethel and Hebron, others from an accidental coincidence, as Emmaus, which was found to be just as far from the new Bethlehem in the New World, as the original Emmaus was from Jerusalem. Nazareth, however, had already been named by John Whitefield, who, after his failure at Savannah, had purchased a superb domain in the forks of the Delaware, to which were attached the right of holding a Court Baron, and other, now extinct, privileges. Before the large stone building, of which he laid the foundation, could be completed, he left the place, and sold his "Manor of Nazareth" to the Moravians. It was from here that the intrepid Zinzendorf, with his loving daughter and a few converted Indians, set out on a pilgrimage through the wilderness, then unexplored and full of peril, and on this occasion he beheld, the first European, the beautiful valley of Wyoming, that was so soon to become the scene of one of the most tragic events in our history. And yet, Moravian records point to an even more disgraceful act, which will probably forever remain a mysterious blot on the American name. For a few years afterwards some Moravians had moved westward, with a few Praying Indians, and settled in the forks of the beautiful Muskingum River, at a place they called Schoenbrunn, Fair Spring, in the midst of Delaware and Mohican Indians, for whose conversion they labored with their usual zeal and touching self-denial. Here dwelt the noble-spirited Logan, so long the friend and at last the victim of the whites; here labored the pious Heckewelder, whose daughter Maria, born April 16, 1781, was the first native "Buckeye." But here also appeared, in the month of March of the following year, a Colonel Williamson, with a body of American troops, and, under the pretext of punishing the treasonable sentiments of the Brethren, surprised, captured and murdered all the inhabitants. Penning up the men in one "slaughter house," and women and children in another, he allowed ninety-six innocent beings to be massacred and scalped! No wonder that the Beautiful Fountain ran with blood and was speedily forsaken, never again to become the home of happy men.

Much might finally be said of the towns in our land, that have, with American fickleness, changed their names, even as men do among us for good or bad, or no reasons at all. The motive seems often to have been incredibly trifling, as was the case with a well-known beautiful village in the State of New York, near the famous falls in the Hudson River. The Indians called it naïvely Che-pon-tuc, a difficult place to get around, as they knew from their experience; then a man from Dutchess County, Abraham Wing, held the land under a grant from the Crown, and the place became known as Wing's Falls. His son, however, in a drinking bout, sold the place, with the right to name it, for a supper; and when the feast was over, the purchaser, John Glenn, instantly posted handbills on all the bridle-paths which then led from the falls to Schenectady and Albany announcing the change in name, and Glen's Falls it has been to the present day. Other cases are of greater interest, but we must content ourselves with noticing two among the many which may fairly serve as types, and, at the same time, enforce the importance which commends such researches to all faithful students of history. Wood, in his well-known New England Retrospect, speaks of a place near the coast which the Indians once upon a time called Misbaumut, but he vouchsafes no explanation, haply not possessing one, and simply adds, that it was also known as Shawmut. This term is fortunately significative and means Sweet Water, and near this place lived one of the many strongly-marked characters of those early days, in which the aim of education was not yet to stamp all men alike with the same mark, that they might thus all become "free and equal." In a solitary cottage, and apparently without any means of support, lived the Rev. W. Blackstone, a minister of the Episcopal Church, and a great thorn in the side of his neighbors. Dr. Mather said of him, sneeringly: This man was of particular humor and would never join himself to any of the New England churches, giving his reason for this, that as he came from England because he did not like the Lord Bishops, so he could not join with them, because he would not be under the Lord Brethren. Nor does this wrath seem to have subsided yet; for Hawthorne, in his charming romance of Merry Mount, represents the reverend gentleman, though with a cautious reservation, as dancing around the May-pole! In an unguarded moment he told his jealous brethren at Charlestown of an excellent spring near his cabin; they immediately came to examine it, they tasted the water, and they determined to have the land. But he was by no means willing to give up so easily what he considered his own. They had to pay him his price, and revenged themselves on him by saying that he demanded money "because he happened to be the first man who stepped on shore!" A settlement was at once made, and the foundation laid for a new town. They named it, in 1633, in honor of the Rev. John Cotton, the "Patriarch of New England," who was their leader, their pastor and their lawgiver. He had been rector at St. Botolph's, in Boston, Lincolnshire, England, and had given up his ample income, his high position and a large part of his devoted flock to cast in his lot with the smaller portion, his fellow-pilgrims, who sought under his guidance a peaceful home among the savages of the New World. He landed on the coast of New England in September, 1633, in company with other eminent divines, whose names, like his own, gave comfort to the poor pilgrims after their own grim and quaint fashion. "We have now," they said, "nothing more to fear, since we have Cotton for our clothing, Hooker for our fishing, and Stone for our building." Thus arose the city of Boston, for a time hesitating between the new name and Tremont, a more classical designation preferred by those who saw in the Tri-mountain City, as they called it, from the three hills on which it stands, a good omen of future greatness. But Boston it remained, and soon rose to such eminence that, in the North, Bostonais became the common French name for all Americans, down to the revolution, and in the far West the remoter Indians to this day have not ceased to call any white man they meet simply a Boston.

The most interesting feature in the history of our great capital is the number of remarkable omens which, under various forms, seem to have foreshadowed the future greatness of the city. That marvellous explorer, whose quaintly simple name we meet everywhere, from the northernmost coasts of New England to the spacious harbors of Virginia, Captain John Smith, was probably the first European who sailed up the River of Swans, the Potomac, to its falls, and in July, 1608, landed on the present site of Washington. He found traditions and evidences alike that the Indians had for many a generation kept here one of their great council-fires, and thus he looked with special interest at the broad bay formed by the noble river. The first name connected with the place is curiously enough that of the "Widow's Mite," under which designation a tract of land, containing 600 acres, and lying "on the East side of Anacostia river, on the North branch or inlet in the said river, called Tiber," was granted to a certain William Langworth, on July 6th, 1661. So untrue was Moore's sneering line, that

"What was Goose Creek once is Tiber now."

A certificate, dated June 5, 1663, describes this land as carefully surveyed and situated at the mouth of a bay or inlet, called Tiber, and from that day no change has taken place in the name of the river. The site, however, became soon after known as Roon, and a city was laid out—

though not built—in 1693, with the same modest rivulet running through its centre. Tradition adds to this fact the information that a Mr. Pope at that time built a house on the place, where the magnificent Capitol now rears its lofty dome, and called it the Capitoline Hill, while he bestowed upon the grounds that surrounded it the name of Rome—perhaps with a slight allusion to his thus becoming the Pope of Rome. Nothing was done, however, besides this prophetic action ; and even when Washington encamped with Braddock's forces on the hill on which the National Observatory now stands, he was almost alone in his enthusiastic admiration of the beautiful site. As if to add another omen to the preceding promises, he actually drew up a plan for a city to be built here, and two towns, Carrollsburg and Hamburg, were really laid out and projected on the present site of Washington. Nor were there other great men wanting to support his excellent judgment, and among them Richard Henry Lee's father, Thomas Lee, one of the leading men of the Atlantic colonies, was especially loud in his praises. He had long turned his attention to the regions lying West of the Alleghanies, and used to say that "he had no doubt America would declare herself independent of Great Britain and the seat of the new government would be near the little falls of the Potomac." He proved the strength of his convictions by acquiring large tracts of land near the falls, which, down to the last generation at least, were still in the possession of his descendants. Thus all seemed to be prepared for the future greatness of the city, and when subsequently David Burns, the proprietor, conveyed his land to the first commissioners appointed for the purpose, the change from the village in the woods to the capital of the Union was vividly represented by the change in the name from the "Widow's Mite" to the "City of Washington.'

KAISERS, KINGS AND KNIGHTS.

V.

N a forlorn, desolate part of our Atlantic coast there lies a lonely island rarely found on general maps, little known in history even, and yet appealing to every feeling of our heart by a sad tragedy which it witnessed long before brave Captain Smith sailed up the King's River or the Mayflower came in sight of Plymouth Rock. Years before, on a warm July night in 1584, two valiant sailors, sent by the great Raleigh, had made land here, and, unfurling the lion flag of the Tudors for the first time in sight of the virgin Continent, had broken the stillness of the evening air with the thunder of a *saker*. Philip Amidas and Arthur Barlow, the two captains, then made their way inland, through crooked inlets and a maze of countless channels, till they reached, twenty miles up the river Occam, an island called Roanoke. But they did not stay long; their minds were fairly overcome with wonder at all they saw; a strange, unknown land, abounding with trees and shrubs never beheld before, forests filled with birds of rich plumage and beasts of marvellous shapes, and above all, men of a red color, clad in savage fashion, but rich in stores of pearls, and eloquent in the praise of neighboring lands where gold and silver were found in profusion. So they gazed their fill, and, ere the summer had passed, bent their course homeward again, reaching England in early September, and astounding the world with countless rumors of new and glorious discoveries. They made their report to Raleigh, delighting his noble heart and filling his soul with ambitious plans and magnificent visions of the future; they deeply interested learned philosophers and astute divines, and finally were sent for to appear at Court and tell the Queen's majesty of the new country and the wild men they had discovered. Elizabeth was highly pleased with the honor thus conferred upon her reign and with the prospect of extending her power over new domains, and ever most liberal where no expense was incurred, she rewarded Raleigh by bestowing upon him knighthood, and honored the newly-discovered land by naming it Virginia. She did this, says an old historian quaintly, " as the greatest mark of honor she could do the discovery," and called it Virginia " as well for that it was first discovered in her reign, a Virgin Queen, as that it did still seem to retain the Virgin purity and plenty of the first creation and the people the primitive innocence." (R. Beverly, Pr. State of Va. p. 3).

Thus it was that Roanoke became the first great and memorable name in our early history. The word meant a special kind of shell-fish, but whether the ill-fated island received its Indian name from the fact that on it were " found great store of muskles " (Hakluyt Voy. III. 3051), or the shells were so called from the locality, is still an open question. We only know that there was " a sort of beads current among the Indians, but of far less value, and this is made of cockle-shell, broke into small bits with rough edges, drilled through in the same manner as beads, and this is called Roenoke and used as the Peak " (Beverly Pr. State of Va. p. 59). Captain John Smith, with his usual marvellous accuracy of facts and utter disregard for sounds, speaks of Raurenock, the common shell-money of the Indians, and adds shrewdly that it was " the occasion of as much discussion among salvages as gold and silver among Christians " (Virginia, p. 158).

A year elapsed, and once more English ships brought English adventurers to the charming regions of the now world-famous island. This time, however, they came prepared to stay; and Ralph Lane, the Governor, having erected a small fort " with sundry decent dwelling-houses " at the northern extremity of the island, wrote the first letter ever sent from distant America to the home-country. It was dated from the " New Fort in Virginia," in " the harborough at Roanoak," and bore date of September 3, 1585. Fortunately it fell into the hands of a great scholar, whose marvellous intelligence foresaw instinctively the priceless value which posterity would attach to the document, and thus it was preserved in his papers and published with other precious relics of those days, as originally addressed to " Master Richard Hackluyt, Esq., of the Middle Temple." Ralph Lane remained with his little band of sailors and soldiers for nearly twelve months on the island, examining "the hundred islands" that dotted the picturesque coast, and sallying forth, every now and then, to search for the fabulous regions far inland, where gold and silver were said to abound, "with ample store of precious pearl." They were a chosen band of noble men, who thus obeyed the impulse given by the great Raleigh, and, at his bidding, went forth to behold the wonders and to secure the treasures of a New World. Never before and never since has a little, lonely island like Roanoke seen such a lordly company, in which matchless valor, profound learning and pure virtue were so happily blended. There was Ralph Lane, soon after to be knighted by the Queen for his many great exploits as a soldier; there was Sir Richard Grenville, one of the master-spirits of his age, who commanded the fleet; Cavendish, the first bold mariner that ever sailed around the globe; with a celebrated painter who transferred the marvels of Virginia faithfully to canvas; and above all, Thomas Hariot, the historian, naturalist and mathematician, whose fame has come down undimmed to our own generation. And yet there was still another man on board the ships that brought this rare assembly of heroes and of scholars, whose name ought to be dearer to us than any of the others. Amidas and Barlow had persuaded an Indian, called by them Manteo, and first mentioned on April 26th, 1585, as "a salvage," simply to accompany them on their homeward journey to England; he had there excited the utmost curiosity and the deepest interest, for he was the first Virginian ever seen in the Old World, and, at the same time, the " friend of the English," a title he had already earned by many a kindly service, and was to deserve still more fully by subsequent deeds. Upon the arrival of Lane he was sent to the main to announce the wishes of the new-comers; he guided them in their restless, eager wanderings; he saved them from many a danger, and more than once from famine and sudden destruction by treacherous tribes, and soon was looked upon by high and low as a friend and a brother. It was he, no doubt, who aided Hariot in studying the virtues of tobacco, which he firmly believed to possess great healing powers, who made known to him the marvellous fruitfulness of maize, and taught him to appreciate the pleasant taste and nutritious qualities of the potato—all of them plants now first made known to the children of the Old World. For a year the English continued on the island of Roanoke, but as the promised precious metals could not be found, as stores became scant and luxuries came to an end, they willingly seized the offer of Sir Francis Drake, whose fleet opportunely appeared " in the wild road of their bad harbor," and embarked for home.

This desertion of the new country caused deep disappointment throughout all England, and only one stout heart remained firm in its fixed purpose. This was Raleigh; undismayed by failure and serious losses, he determined instantly to repair the misfortune and to send out a new colony, well fitted to form a permanent settlement on his favorite island. The month of July, of the same year, 1587, saw a third fleet of brave Englishmen land on Roanoke Island, and among them the first woman that beheld the New World. In Sir Walter Raleigh's "indenture of grant," dated 17th January, 1587, John White and eleven others are directed to go to "the lately discovered barbarous land and countries, called Assamacomack, or Wingandocoia, or Virginia," (Oldy's Life of Sir W. Raleigh), and in April the new Governor, with 117 men, women and children, set out on his ill-fated voyage. They landed once more on the island; they met once more their faithful friend and ally Manteo, "that behaved himself towards us as a most faithful Englishman," and induced the Indians, who at first seemed determined to prevent a landing, "to throw away their armes" and to be friends. Their first welcome, however, was sad; and who can wonder that their hearts were at once filled with evil forebodings? Sir Richard Grenville, unwilling that his countrymen should lose the newly-won country entirely, had left fifteen brave men on the island, to be the guardians of English rights. For these the new settlers looked with eagerness and deepest interests; but Manteo, when questioned about them, was ominously silent, and when they reached the fort they found the cabins in ruins, the gardens browsed by wild deer and the ground strewn with bleached bones! Their hearts sank within them, and all the beauty of nature and all the exuberant richness of the soil could not efface the ineffable sorrow that had fallen upon their souls at the dismal sight.

Their forebodings were but too soon to be fulfilled.

At first all went on well, and great was the joy and bright were the hopes of the English, when the foundations of the great city of Raleigh were laid at the place where a fort had been built by Ralph Lane, and the mother and kindred of Manteo welcomed them solemnly and cordially to their new home. The month of August, especially, was ripe with stately ceremonies and happy events. On the thirteenth of that month Manteo, the "faithful Englishman," was baptized, and at the special command of the proprietary of Virginia, Sir W. Raleigh, clothed with the full rank and honors of a feudal baron. All the formalities of such an investiture that were possible under the circumstances were scrupulously observed; the new peer was solemnly invested with the dignity of "Lord of Roanoke and Baron of Dassamonpeach, in token of his faithfulnesse," and thus Virginia and all America beheld the first—and only—peerage ever bestowed upon a son of the soil (Bancroft Hist. of the U. S., I. p. 105). It is not a little curious that the only man who ever bore the same title in a more modest fashion claimed with good right to be a descendant of the great Emperor of Virginia, for John Randolph of Roanoke, so called to distinguish him from his kinsmen, the Randolphs of Tuckahoe, Dungeness and Cures, traced his pedigree back to Powhatan, the father of Pocahontas.

Unfortunately no further trace can be found of the first native nobleman in the annals of our land; he probably valued the well-meant honor as little as Powhatan did the royal crown sent him from England, and soon exchanged it for the more substantial dignity of Werowanee of his own nation.

One more bright gleam of sunshine lighted up the hearts of the colonists of Roanoke, before that dark gloom fell upon them, which has hid them forever from the eye of man. On the 18th of the same month the Governor's daughter, who had married Ananias Dare, one of the assistants, presented him with a child, which, being the first Christian infant born on this Continent, was baptized on the following Sunday and called Virginia. (Hakluyt Voy. III. 345). The student of history, who loves to notice quaint features and strange combinations in our early annals, cannot fail to be struck by the curious importance which seems to have been accidentally attached to the name of White in our history. Here was John White's grand-daughter, the first offspring of English parents on the soil of America. The first child born of English parents in New England was Peregrine White, the son of Susanna White, who gladdened the eyes of his father on board the Mayflower, as she lay, towards the close of November, 1620, in the harbor of Plymouth. Even the Catholic Church, denying to so many of her children the joys of paternity, seems to have put in her claims to the favored name, for it was a Father White, who, as chaplain to Leonard Calvert, in the year 1633, planted a cross and said holy mass near St. Mary's, and thus first consecrated the soil of the Land of the Sanctuary, the Terra Mariae.

Soon after this happy event, the Governor, yielding to the urgent prayers of the timid colonists, sailed for home, in order to procure for them supplies and reinforcements, leaving behind him, with anxious heart, a hundred and eight souls that had been intrusted to his care, and among them, precious pledges, his daughter and his grand-child, Virginia Dare. Could he have foreseen the delays, the troubles, the dangers even, that awaited him in England, he would never have abandoned the infant colony, he would never have parted with those that were dearest to him on earth. But Fate had decreed it otherwise. It was only in 1590 that he could return to the island, but who can describe his anguish when he found the place utterly deserted; who can follow him in his maddening efforts to recover his beloved ones! With the calm of despair, in touching, simple words, he tells us: "We went up and down the Ile; at last we found three faire Roman letters carved, C. R. O., which presently we knew to signifie the place where I should find them according to a secret note between them and me. But we found no sign of distresse—then we went to a place where they were left in sundry houses, but we found them all taken downe and the place strongly inclosed with a high Palisade, very Fort-like, and in one of the chiefe posts carved in fayre capitall Letters: Croatan." (Master John White's Report, 1590.)

Thus ended the brief and sad history of the island that first saw Christian settlers and first gave its name to be a title to an American nobleman. His domain never held town or farm—only English graves. The mystery of the Continent had been broken by the bold explorers, but another mystery had promptly taken its place, never to be revealed to human eye. For the poor settlers had vanished, leaving no trace behind them save the mysterious name, Croatan, now borne by a part of the ill-fated island. At the beginning of the century the remains of the tree were still pointed out to the curious traveller, on which the fatal word had been carved, and the Indians, with their usual tenacity in clinging to local traditions, have ever unerringly kept the remembrance of the site on which Master Ralph Lane built his stronghold and Raleigh hoped to found the city that bore his name. A gaunt, live oak, weather-beaten and bearing the traces of many a fierce tempest, stands now sentinel in the centre of the old bastion, a fit emblem in winter of the woe it once was fated to behold, and decked in summer with a thousand green vines, speaking eloquently of happier days to come. A like vague trace may possibly be found of the lonely settlers who once perhaps gathered around the sapling. Indian traditions speak of descendants of the first colonists as still living among their brethren in North Carolina. For Manteo, they say, a " faithful Englishman " to the end, and mindful of the solemn oath he had sworn as Lord of Roanoke, took the white men with their wives and children, to save them from being brutally murdered, to his own distant tribe; there they dwelt and married and died, their children being adopted among the Hatteras, and to this day careful observers firmly believe that traces of white blood may be clearly seen in the features and forms of these Indians.

It was not till many generations had passed away that Virginia once more knew a Lord, who was one of her own citizens, and not merely an official sent by the home government to rule the colony. From time of old the noble family of Fairfax seems to have had a liking for the Old Dominion, for already, in 1632, when the king made profuse grants of land there, free from quit-rents and carrying with them the rights of sovereign authority, the first " Lord Fairfax held a Court baron " in Virginia (Burk. Hist. of Va. II. 38, note). It is not stated, however, that the great parliamentary general ever came over to enjoy his privileges or that the grant descended to his children. But when Charles II. imitated his father's example, and, with equal disregard to the interests of the State and the rights of actual settlers, gave away millions of acres in many a single grant, the bond between the ancient family of the Fair Hair and the oldest colony of the crown in England was once more renewed. In the year 1697 the reckless monarch bestowed upon his two favorites, Lord Colepeper (for so he signed his name) and the Earl of Arlington nothing less than " all the dominion of land and water called Virginia !" James II, on ascending the throne, made a new, full grant of the whole territory to the Culpeper family in 1682, and through him it passed to the Fairfax. For the Lord Culpeper of those days had a fair daughter, of whom he wrote in a letter addressed to his sister, and dated from Boston, New England, October 5, 1680: " I shall now marry Cate as soone as I can, and shall then reckon myselfe to be a Freeman without clogge or charge. T. Clp'r." He succeeded admirably in ridding himself of the "clogge," for the beautiful heiress became soon after the wife of Thomas, the fifth Lord Fairfax, and brought him, as part of her ample dower, a tract of land in Virginia, called the Northern Neck, and containing nearly six millions of acres. This magnificent domain, bounded by the two rivers Potomac and Rappahannock, and extending from the Atlantic Ocean to the head waters of the latter in the Blue Ridge, and of the former in the Alleghanies, fell, in 1710, to his eldest son, Thomas, together with several manors in Kent, and rich estates in the Isle of Wight. He began life with all the prestige that noble birth, ample fortune and unusual personal attractions could afford; but the splendor of his military career and high rank, the flattering success of his contributions to the *Spectator*, and the renown he soon acquired at court and in town as a wit, could not console him when his fondest hopes were disappointed. His deeply-wounded heart sought consolation in foreign travel, and as he came from a good republican stock he naturally turned to the freer life and greater independence of the colonies. Thus he came to his magnificent domain in Virginia, and was so delighted with the great beauty of the land and the charms of society that he resolved to spend the remainder of his life there, though then not yet fifty years of age. For many years he lived at Belvoir, his superb country seat near Mount Vernon, and it was here that, in 1748, he first became acquainted with George Washington, then sixteen years old, and conceived for him an affection which soon ripened and was warmly returned. He was so much struck with the energetic and reliable character of the young man that he intrusted to him at once the responsible and often dangerous duty of surveying his lands in the beautiful Valley of Virginia. The enthusiasm with which the generally impassive American spoke of the lovely valleys and rich lands lying West of the blue Ridge excited the interest of the English peer; he went to see for himself and found the land even fairer than it had been represented. He built himself at once a mansion in a beautiful manor of ten thousand acres, which he appropriately called Greenway Court, and here led the quiet but apparently happy life of a country-gentleman, delighting in field sports of every kind and dispensing the most profuse liberality to all who would visit his house. Plain and simple in his dress, modest and unaffected in his manners, his generosity alone was truly magnificent. To his brother Robert, who afterwards succeeded him in the peerage, he gave up all his noble estates in England, while in Virginia no neighbor or new settler ever came to his house in want of land on whom he did not promptly bestow enough to make him a home for life. Nor did the noble lord ever forget for a moment that he was also a citizen of the Colonial Commonwealth: he attended court regularly at the county town, twelve miles off, acting as presiding judge and keeping open table during the session, and performed with the same scrupulous fidelity the humble duties of Keeper of the Rolls of Frederick County, in which he lived. Eccentric in views and ways, he spent half his time in the fields and forests with his dogs and his horses, the daily routine being only interrupted when distinguished visitors reached Greenway Court. Among these perhaps the most frequent and always the most welcome was George Washington, who joined with enthusiasm in his hunting-parties, and ever listened with deference to his opinions, even when at a later period the English peer tried to dissuade the American patriot from pursuing the war. It would be difficult to say who was more honored by this mutual forbearance, the loyal lord or the wise captain. When Braddock's defeat laid the fair lands of the valley open to incursions from the Indians, the white-haired old Baron placed himself bravely at the head of a troop of horse, and sternly refused to leave his forest-home in spite of threatening dangers and urgent advice from all his friends. Nor did he waver for a moment when the revolution broke out, and all around him, endeared neighbors, life-long friends and near kinsmen joined the cause of freedom and left him to sigh and sorrow in his lonely, childless home. He could bear the seclusion, the abandonment and the courteous forbearance with which he was allowed to live unmolested in his seclusion, but when the cause of his king and his country was utterly lost, the proud lord's heart was broken, and he went to his fathers, having nearly completed a century of wayward but honorable life.

The spirit of a free country is fatal to titles of honor as well as to estates of unfair proportions. This was strikingly illustrated in the history of the Lords Fairfax.

The title, in absence of direct heirs for two or three generations, went almost begging to uncles and nephews, and would perhaps be entirely forgotten by the great world but for the record in Burke and Debrett. The magnificent estate long managed by the lord's kinsman, William Fairfax, of Belvoir, whose daughter married the elder brother of George Washington, and thus inaugurated a long line of intermarriages between the two families, dwindled away year after year, till now no trace is to be found of the princely domain. The reckless manner in which in those days fertile districts and rich territories were given and bartered away appears now almost sinful. Thus one of Lord Fairfax's early agents, a man by the name of Burden, had the good fortune of procuring a young buffalo calf while surveying his master's lands on the beautiful Shenandoah. He presented the strange animal to Governor Gooch, and received in return a grant of half a million acres "either on the Shenandoah or James River," on the sole condition of settling a hundred families there within ten years! (De Hass. Hist. of Ind. Wars, p. 39). The lands are still known as Burden's Grant, and much of it is yet in the possession of his descendants. But the agent was in this case more fortunate than his employer. For already, in 1794, the great Northern Neck Grant had dwindled down to 9700 acres, the whole of which was offered to a Mr. Carter, of Shirley, at forty shillings (Virginia currency) an acre!

Thus it seems that in those early days—as for many generations afterwards—the active agent invariably prospered, while the indolent owner of large estates went on wasting his estates and neglecting his interests. But the whole history of the Old Dominion presents no more striking instance of this strange but almost unfailing change of fortune than the succession of Lord Fairfax by King Carter.

Not far from the banks of the Rappahannock River, where it spreads its beautiful waters as far as eye can reach, and is bordered by lands of surpassing richness and marvellous beauty, there stood once a stately church, built of English brick, and richly adorned with abundance of carving, with ample windows and costly damask curtains, all specially imported from the Old Country. It rose in massive strength and fair proportions in the centre of a noble grove of trees, and its silvery bell rang far over land and water. And as its summons were heard, carriages approached on high-road and by-ways, boats were seen dashing rapidly up and down the gentle river, and on many a thorough-bred came swain and damsel, holding each other in timid embrace. But as they alighted in the grove, they ranged themselves, high and low, young and old, by the side of the massive entrance door, exchanging kindly greetings in an undertone, and glancing every now and then at the stately avenue of trees that led across the hill to the owner's mansion. At last two out-riders in gay livery appeared on the summit, half hid in a cloud of dust, then rose the outlines of a great coach and four, with wigged coachman and powdered lackeys; it drew up near the church, and, a moment after, a stout, cheerful looking man appeared, leading a fair lady, whose gloved hand daintily touched his arm. A whole bevy of servants, wearing their master's colors, followed him at some little distance, and, first of all who had assembled, he entered the sacred building. The little choir gathered in haste, the organ pealed forth the introitus, the minister arose from his chair, and soon the church was filled. There sat King Carter, as he was universally called, the lord of the manor, in his richly curtained and padded family pew; there were his tenants, filling one half of the spacious floor, and behind him up to the door his livery servants and farm hands. As he had generously built the old church in place of a smaller one erected by one of his ancestors as early as 1670, on his own land, and out of his private purse, and still continued to bear all the expenses, no one complained of the large space he required, but most willingly did homage to the large-hearted, high-minded donor. There was no irony in the name they had bestowed upon him : if he was a king among them by the vast size of his domains, the immense wealth he possessed, and the great power he wielded by his wisdom as well as by his influence in high places, he was famous also for his royal bounty and the matchless generosity which characterized him in all his transactions.

In England it is the king who makes the peer—here in Virginia it had been the peer who made the king. For Robert Carter had long been the agent and representative of the two noble families of Culpeper and Fairfax in the distant colony, and had in course of time become the real proprietor of the princely domain of the Northern Neck, though still paying the lordly owner an annual rent of three hundred pounds. In his own right he owned, besides, three hundred thousand acres of land and eleven hundred slaves—by far the largest fortune ever owned by private citizen in the old commonwealth. Nor had political preferments long waited to seek the shrewd business-man, the wise counsellor: he was, at least for one year, governor of the colony; and then, for his lifetime, president of the King's Council, and Secretary of Virginia. There is something almost ludicrous in the but half-concealed awe with which his honors and titles, his wealth and his lands, are spoken of by William Strachey, Gent, first Secretary of the colony, in his " Historie of Travaile into Virginia Brittanica." Apparently by an accident—though not perhaps altogether without a slight purpose—we are let into the secret of one source of the king's wonderful success in life. When he was Secretary of the Colony, it appears it was his duty to assign land-grants and to dispose of the still available regions in what was then called Western Virginia, the land at the foot and West of the Blue Ridge. A claimant would present himself in his office and make known to him his wish to obtain possession of some rich bottom or well-watered pasture. Apparently doubtful as to its true condition, King Carter would call to his clerk in an adjoining room to see if the desired lands were yet taken up or not. The answer came promptly: if the land was poor, the claimant was gratified at once by receiving his patent; but if it was rich and well situated, Robert Carter's name was instantly entered, and the poor applicant punished for the candor with which he had informed the Secretary of the value of his claim. Thus the king came to own a large portion of the most valuable land in all Virginia; among them the long, low mountain range with its rich and beautiful slopes, which still retains his name, and on its Northern extremity bears the home of Jefferson. Was it the memory of these and similar transactions in his busy, prosperous life, or was it mock modesty and rollicking recklessness, that made him write his own epitaph thus :

> Here lies Robin, but not Robin Hood,
> Here lies Robin, who ne'er did good,
> Here lies Robin, whom God has forsaken,
> Here lies Robin, whom the Devil has taken.

The real epitaph, which, after his death, in 1732, was placed over his grave at the eastern end of the church, is in its quaint Latin redolent with sincere praise, and closes with the touching, truthful words: " The poor lament, having lost their comforter, the widows their protector, the orphans their father."

The noble church, King Carter's worthiest monument, still stands on the banks of the York; its stout walls, three feet thick, are uninjured, its windows unharmed, its old marble font, the most beautiful in all Virginia, still stands before the first communion-table ever used, and even the old cedar dial posts, on which the name of John Carter, the king's father, is carved, with the date of the year 1702, has been preserved to this day. But "riches certainly make themselves wings," and the fate of the peer's magnificent domain has also been that of the king's great estate. The eccentricity that often cropped out in the life of the latter was inherited by his descendants, and perhaps not always held in check by the same good judgment and practical wisdom. Already his grandson, Counsellor Carter, of Nomini, astonished and shocked the world by becoming first a zealous Anabaptist, building even a chapel on his manor for the forbidden sect, then an enthusiastic Swedenborgian, and seeking finally rest for his mind and peace for his soul in the Church of Rome. The broad acres of the king were squandered, divided out and forfeited, till nothing is now left of his superb domain, and his kinsmen of our day seek distinction in virtues and merits that are better than " riches and great possessions."

While Virginia had her genuine lord and her king of the Colony, South Carolina could boast of the only order of nobility that was ever legally instituted within the limits of the Republic. Nor is it the least interesting feature in this memorable scheme that the first Landgrave of Carolina was no less a person than the great philosopher Locke. It is well known how the latter, when a youthful student of medicine, had accidentally cured Lord Ashley of a dangerous disease, and how gratitude and esteem had gradually bound the two friends to each other in close union. When many years afterwards the nobleman had, as Earl of Shaftesbury, received with seven other persons a grant of the whole province of Carolina, he requested his friend to draw up a code of fundamental laws for his new domain. The famous constitution was a marvel of theoretical beauty and perfect method ; it commends our admiration even at this day for its bold avowal and practical enforcement of religious liberty, and for the extreme ingenuity displayed in its cautious mixture of aristocratic institutions with popular laws. But practically it was a simple impossibility, and hence its life was short. Its Landgraves, hereditary lords with four barons under them, and its Caciques with two barons, never found an opportunity to meet in their proposed Colonial Parliament, and, except for the mere sake of distinction, no use was ever made of the high-sounding titles, as no effect was ever given to their official powers. There is almost a stroke of poetical policy in the curious fact that the only Landgrave, of whom history ever speaks, bore the plebeian name of Smith. He was about to leave the province, in the year 1692, in utter disgust with its ill-fated constitution and its unsafe condition, when a terrible storm drove an unlucky brigantine to seek shelter in the harbor of Charleston, under lee of Sullivan's Island. The crew, exhausted by a long voyage from Madagascar, was on the point of perishing, when the generous Landgrave went on board to provide for their wants. By chance he noticed a little bag in the cook's caboose, with a few odd-looking white grains in it, and was surprised to learn that that was rice. The little treasure-trove was at once presented to him by the grateful Malay, and he, in his turn, distributed the precious seed among his friends, adding such directions as to their treatment as he had taken pains to obtain himself from the dusky cook. They were planted in gardens and throve; they were set out in fields the following years, and brought rich crops, and thus the few little grains gave rise to the culture of rice, which now makes up largely the wealth of the State and keeps alive the memory of Thomas Smith, the Landgrave of South Carolina.

While Virginia had her Emperor, as Captain Smith always insisted upon calling the Chief of the Powhatans, and her society bestowed royal dignity upon the Marquis of Carabas of her early days, and long before Carolina boasted of Landgraves and Caciques, a Northern State witnessed a ludicrous effort to establish a new aristocracy and the first knightly order ever known to our land. There may be found in some of our best libraries a most rare, quaint-looking volume, one of the great puzzles of historians, and a dainty tit-bit for lovers of odd conceits. The author bears—or assumes—the high-sounding title of Beauchamp Plantagenet of Beloil, and calls his pamphlet, printed in 1648 : " A Description of the Province of New Albion in North America." On the second page of the little book there appear the "medall and riban" of the new order of the " Albion Knights of the Conversion of Twenty-Three kings," a copy of their arms and supporters, and the unpoetical motto :

> All power of life and death, the Sword and Crown,
> On Gospel's truth shine Honor and Renown.

The coat of arms, magnificently emblazoned according to strictest rules of heraldry contains a portrait of the twenty-two decapitated kings in the forms of so many "heads couped and crowned," held up by the twenty-third, who kneels down before them in savage costume and supports the shield. The head of this famous order of knights was no less a personage than the Earl Palatine, of New Albion, known in Shropshire, England, as modest Sir Edmund Plowden, and little regarded in Boston, where he sought help to establish his dominion, but found no sympathy with his knightly aspirations. Titles and surnames were all made ready for not less than forty-four lords, baronets and knights; noble seats were provided for the head of the order, the most remarkable of which was "Mount Ployden, the seat of the Raritan king, a square rock a hundred and fifty feet high, the retired Paradise of the children of the Ethiopian Emperor," and others for the remaining knights—in fact the whole armor was prepared, from the crest on the helmet to the golden spur on the heel; but no one was found willing to assume the strange garb and to convert the "twenty-three Indian kings." It was at a time doubted whether the whole story was not perhaps a mere hoax or a clever swindle to allure colonists and sell lands in the distant colony—the scheme was so very extravagant and the Order so very fantastic. But on "a Mapp of Virginia discovered to ye Hills &c. Domina Virginia Farrer Collegit. Are sold by I. Stephenson at ye farme below Ludgate, 1651," New Albion is really entered in the neighborhood of what is now known as New Jersey, and on "Lord Delaware's Bay" this remark is made: "This River Lord Ployden hath a patent of and calls it New Albion, but the Swedes are planted in it and have a great trade of furs." And so it really was : the patent existed, Sir E. Plowden owned it, and New Albion was the name of his domain. But the explanation of the apparent mystery is given in Winthrop's History of England, which states that Sir E. Plowden came landless and penniless to Boston in 1648. "He came first with a patent of a county Palatine for Delaware Bay, but wanting a pilot for the place, he went to Virginia, and there having lost the estate he brought over, and all his people scattered from him, he came hither to return to England for supplies." Thus ended the first effort to establish an Order of Knights in our land, and the "twenty-three Indian kings" we fear were never converted.

The next attempt—hardly deserving the name—was a pitiless joke, played at the expense of a vain Frenchman. Among the early officials in New France few were better known in Court circles at home than a brave but weak soldier, the Sieur de la Motte Cadillac. His place in American history is one of no small distinction, for after having earned considerable renown in many a bloody battle at home and abroad, we hear of him starting, in 1701, from Montreal, with a hundred men and a "Black Gown," as the Jesuits were universally called, to punish certain refractory Indian tribes. On this expedition he built a fort and established a settlement at a prominent point in the river or strait of St. Clare near its connection with Lake Erie. The place became first known as the fort d'Etroit, soon to be merged in the city of Detroit, and Cadillac has thus the merit of having laid the first foundations of the State of Michigan. In France he was far more widely and more popularly known by his letters, written to his patron, the famous Duke of Lauzun. They were full of the most naïve avowals of every kind of weakness with which human nature may be charged, and abounded in blunders in word and in thought. Whenever one of these epistles arrived from distant Canada, the clever courtier would take it with him to the levee, and, seizing a favorable moment, read it to the king. The unconscious ignorance, the matchless stupidity and the intense self-conceit they displayed, all were forcibly brought out by the witty prince, and they never failed to amuse Louis, and to cause shouts of laughter among the bystanders. No one wondered, therefore, when some time afterwards Cadillac's application to be made Governor of Louisiana was warmly supported by the ambitious favorite. "What divine letters, what priceless blunders we shall have from Biloxi!" said Lauzun; the king smiled and the appointment was made. Cadillac left without regret the cheerless forests of Canada, though not before securing by every legal form and title the valuable grants of land he had received on the waters of Frenchman's Bay, and sailed for his new government. Months passed and nothing was received in Paris but bitter complaints and tedious remonstrances. But at last a letter came that made ample amends and caused universal and lasting amusement at Court. It appeared that the good people of Louisiana had very soon discovered the weakness of their new governor and became impatient of his foolish orders and absurd demands. Courteous remonstrances and urgent requests had all proved in vain. But when Cadillac finally withdrew from the city in high displeasure, and from his fort issued an order that no one should henceforth be allowed to wear a sword unless he had first proved his right to do so by noble descent or high official standing, they determined to have their revenge. A deputation of prominent and influential men was sent to him, to lay before him for his approval the statutes of a new order of nobility, which they desired to establish, so that the colony also might, under his illustrious government, have its knights, its ribbons and decorations. Cadillac himself was humbly requested to accept the office of Grand Master of the New Order. He assented graciously, and immediately sat down to inform his patron of the great event and the signal honor the colony had chosen to bestow upon him, out of respect for his great talents and lofty virtues. The letter was written in his usual inflated style, related minutely all forms and details of the new knighthood, and closed with the naïve confession that its name was : The Illustrious Order of the Golden Calf! All the solemn majesty effected by Louis XIV. could not resist the matchless humor of the simple-minded governor, and the good people of Louisiana had their revenge. It need hardly be added that the new order was allowed to perish very soon ; but the memory of Cadillac's knighthood has not been effaced. Nor did he allow himself to be entirely forgotten at the North. For as late as 1785 there appeared in Massachusetts a Mme. de Grégoire, who proved her direct descent from the renowned governor, and claimed, in his right, the island of Mount Desert and a large tract of land in the neighborhood. The matter was duly examined, and in 1786 the good lady's claim was duly acknowledged and confirmed (James Sullivan, Hist. of Mass., p. 58).

Very nearly at the same time, another, though more serious, effort was made in Virginia to establish there also an American order of knighthood. The beautiful range of mountains which divides the great State throughout its whole width, leaving the Piedmont and sea-board region on the east, and the great Valley of Virginia on the west, had long attracted the curiosity of explorers and the cupidity of adventurers. Though by no means of Alpine height, the Blue Ridge for many generations formed an apparently insurmountable barrier, and the unknown land beyond, heard of only through vague rumors and fanciful descriptions, became an Eldorado in the minds of the multitude. A Colonel Wood, it is true, was said to have crossed the Alleghanies in 1670, already bent upon trade. At least we are told that " Colonel Wood, inhabiting at the falls of James River, about a hundred miles west of Chesapeake Bay, discovered at several times several branches of the great rivers Ohio and Mechasebe " (D. Coxe, Carolina, p. 113), but no account of his travels is on record, and no practical result was obtained from this enterprise. A few years later Sir William Berkeley had sent a Captain Batte, with a brave little company of fourteen Englishmen and as many Indians, to cross the mountains and to explore the unknown regions beyond. They ascended the first heights and were amply rewarded for their toil by finding here also wide plains and green savannahs, alive with flocks of wild fowl and herds of deer and buffalo, but before them rose new mountains, more rugged even and fuller of precipices than any they had yet ascended. The timid Indians refused to go further, and told wondrous stories of fierce tribes dwelling beyond, who made salt, and never allowed strangers to return when they once had entered their land.

It was no slight undertaking, therefore, when a later Governor, Alexander Spotswood, determined at all hazards to cross the formidable barrier and to explore the mysteries they had so long shrouded from the eyes of men. There was much in his character and much in his previous history to fit him specially for such an adventure. Born of Scottish parents in Tangiers, on the African coast, he had been trained from childhood up in camps and bivouacs. Rising by his valor only, for he had neither birth nor rank to aid him, he was severely wounded fighting under the great Marlborough at Blenheim, and as a reward for his bravery and signal services appointed Lieutenant-Governor of Virginia. With indefatigable zeal and excellent judgment he devoted himself to the development of all the resources of the colony, and thus also conceived the plan of exploring the Alleghanies. He was fully aware of the trials in store and the dangers he would have to encounter; the pathless wilderness bristled with towering rocks and huge precipices; wild beasts infested the mountains, and fierce Indians guarded with savage jealousy the few passes that led to the valleys beyond.

But he knew how to kindle the enthusiasm he himself felt in the breasts of others also; the Assembly lent its aid, and hardly was his purpose made public, in 1710, when chivalrous youths from far and near flocked to the Middle Plantation to enroll themselves under their renowned leader. They felt all the romance of being the first to encounter "the Apalachian Mountains," as it was the fashion in those days to call them; they burnt with an eager desire to see the far-famed regions beyond, and they felt, at the same time, no small satisfaction at the thought that they might thus foil the cunning plans of the French, whose policy it had long been to keep all the country beyond concealed from the English. It was a goodly show when the gallant band of cavaliers, with their gay retinue, set out on their romantic enterprise, at their head a well-tried warrior, and before them a new world full of wonders and strange adventures. Thanks to the prudence of their leader and the imposing array of their forces they met with no serious impediment: their enthusiasm easily overcame all natural obstacles, and their formidable appearance kept the Indians everywhere in check. The season was one full of hope and of promise, and the landscape smiled in all the freshness of early spring upon the gay cavalcade. The first birds of spring were filling the forests with their early love-song; the redbud and dogwood were here and there putting forth their white and purple flowers, contrasting in marvellous beauty with the exquisite, tender green of the young tulip poplar leaves. The steep Alleghany hillsides glowed in the morning light, as the first rays of the sun fell upon the velvet carpet of rich grasses and the deep red gullies washed by the heavy rains, while below the swift rivers swept by, swollen by the melting snows and frequent April showers. The adventurers lingered in many a secluded vale; they were often delayed by an impetuous mountain torrent or an impassable precipice; but at last all obstacles were overcome and they stood on the summit of the great mountain range. They felt at once that whatever toil and trouble they might have encountered they were amply repaid for all by the matchless beauty and imposing grandeur of the scene before them. There, at their feet, as far as their eye could reach, stretched out a vast champagne country, rich in all the best gifts of nature—a boundless domain, promising ample support and a thousand homes to coming generations. Spotswood, with his own hand, carved the name of his king on the highest rock of the mountain, which he called Mount George, and one of his devoted followers gave by a like act the name of Mount Alexander to the next highest summit. Then the merry band returned in triumph to their eastern homes. They had made the first certain discovery of a feasible passage across those mountains and broken forever the charm that had so long kept the English from extending their rule beyond the enchanted barrier. The governor "returned," says the old historian, "with a glory in those times little inferior to that of Hannibal" (Burk. Hist. of Va., I. p. 331), and received in the colony loud applause and warm admiration, and at the hands of his grateful monarch the honor of knighthood.

But it was his desire and the wish of his brave followers to continue in Virginia also the memory of the great exploit, and thus he established an Order of Knighthood, not only for those who had accompanied him, but also all who should hereafter seek distinction and honor in like manner. He called it the Transmontane Order of the Knights of the Golden Horseshoe. The motto, referring to the origin of the order, ran thus: *Sic juvat transcendere montes;* the emblem was a small golden horseshoe, worn on a short, scarlet ribbon. The device was chosen because horse-shoes, little known in Eastern Virginia, which is comparatively free from stones, became of the utmost importance when travelling over rocky mountain heights, and had here, for the first time in the history of Virginia, to be provided in considerable numbers. All the romance of the adventure, and all the attractions of new titles and dignities were, however, unable to compete successfully with the fatality which, from the beginning, seems to have defeated every effort of the kind in this country. The discovery remained fruitless, the explorer was rewarded with bitter ingratitude, and the order of knighthood was soon forgotten. For more than a generation no attempt was made to cross the mountains again, and even the bold enterprise of John Howard, who, in 1742, followed the well-known pathways of deer and elk, and finally, in a canoe made of buffalo skin, sailed down the Ohio, was long considered as little more than a myth. It was mentioned by Kerchcoal (Valley of Va., p. 67), and at a later period by Du Pratz (Lond. ed., 1774) who stated that Howard was taken by the French on the Mississippi, thus securing to him unconsciously the honor of being the first Englishman whose visit to the West, though resulting in no settlement, is distinctly authenticated. The enterprising governor, often described as "A. Spottiswoode," received little thanks from the home government and was even refused compensation for his heavy outlay of money. He retired, soon after the exploit, from political life, and spent his days at Germanna, his country-seat in a county of Virginia, called after him Spotsylvania, and extending westward "to the river beyond the high mountains" (Act of Ass., 1720). Here he was visited by the well-known Colonel Byrd, who humorously describes his residence thus: "This famous town consists of Governor Spotswood's enchanted castle on one side of the street, and a baker's dozen of ruined tenements on the other, where so many German families had dwelt some years ago. There had also been a chapel about a bowshot from the Colonel's house, at the end of an avenue of cherry trees, but some pious people had lately burnt it down, with intent to have one built nearer to their own houses" (Western MSS., p. 131). The knights of the Golden Horseshoe were never mentioned again in the Annals of Virginia.

The last and most recent order of knighthood, belonging not to colonial times, but to the days in which republican principles would seem to have had most influence, has hardly yet existed long enough to allow us to judge of its usefulness. It is well known that some memorial of the perils, the privations and the triumphs of the War of Independence was ardently desired by the officers of the army, especially by the many foreigners who had bravely fought by the side of their American brethren. Washington did not at first encourage the efforts made for that purpose : he was too great, too wise and too modest to appreciate outward distinctions, but he yielded readily to the fondness which all soldiers exhibit for such decorations and to the merit of certain benevolent features which were to be grafted upon the order. At the headquarters of General Steuben on the Hudson River, a meeting was finally held on May 13th, 1783, and here it was proposed and agreed that " The officers of the American Army, having generally been taken from the citizens of America, possess high veneration for the character of the illustrious Roman, Lucius Quintus Cincinnatus, and being resolved to follow his example, by returning to their citizenship, they think they may with propriety denominate themselves The Society of Cincinnati." The great Roman was, of course, only the image of their beloved leader, who himself became the first president ; he was, at his death, succeeded by Hamilton and then by the Pinckneys. Well-chosen emblems were devised, and skilfully made in France, for badges and ornaments, showing mainly the American eagle ; and blue and white colors for the ribbon, in compliment to the combined arms, the French and the American, by which the independence of the States had been secured. At first hereditary, the Order became, in obedience to public sentiment, at least in practice, elective, and continued in vigor till the second visit of Lafayette, who was its only surviving major-general. Extinct in several States, branches of the order still exist in others, though not one of the original members is now living. The order was always much less appreciated at home than abroad, where monarchical governments have learnt to derive great advantages from such decorations; with us it produced no effect at all upon society, and will probably, ere long, survive only in the name of the Queen City, which in January, 1790, received the name of Cincinnata (not, as now, Cincinnati,) from Symmes and St. Clair, " in honor of the order of the Cincinnati, and to denote the chief place of their residence."

Among the royal and noble personages who appear meteor-like in the annals of our early days, two mysterious adventurers must not be forgotten, whose true history remains to this day a puzzle to historians, and a favorite topic of discussion with lovers of secrets.

As early as the year 1668, when British rule was yet paramount in all the colonies and provinces of this continent, there appeared on the banks of the Delaware a young man who soon attracted very general attention by his uncommon personal beauty, his winning manners and rare acquirements. He visited all the wealthier settlers, and was, after the manner of the day, everywhere hospitably entertained, and urged to stay as long as he liked. He called himself Count Königsmark, and claimed to be brother to the far-famed lover of Sophie Dorothea, who was brutally murdered in the castle of Ahlden in presence of the Elector, afterwards George I. of England, and of Aurora, the fair favorite of another Elector, the mother of Maurice of Saxe. His high breeding and his familiarity with court matters in England, as well as in his native land, Sweden, made the claim appear natural; besides, he was amply provided with means, and travelled with a certain degree of stately splendor. The only vulnerable point was his strange familiarity with a man who bore the name of Henry Coleman, but was almost uniformly designated by the common people as "the Fin." The apparent bond between the high-born nobleman and his very humble friend was the fact that they were both natives of Finland; but, besides this, there seemed to be nothing they could possibly have in common. And yet they were continually seen, conferring in close intimacy now with the Swedish settlers on the banks of the river, and now with the Indians still to be found in the neighborhood. The noble Count explained this intercourse as the result of his desire to obtain himself all the information he wished to procure about his country, its present advantages, and future prospects. What could induce "the Fin" to spend all the time which he did not devote to his illustrious countryman in the huts of the Swedes and the wigwams of the savages was known to no one, and caused much wondering and guessing. All of a sudden Conningsmarke, as his name was then written (Proud. Hist. of Pa., p. 128), was arrested, and warrants issued for the apprehension of his friend also. The latter, however, who spoke several Indian languages, had probably been warned in time, and escaped.

In the trial it appeared that the foreign nobleman had been for some time engaged in nothing less than a conspiracy with Swedes and Indians to raise a rebellion for the purpose of throwing off the yoke of the English, and establishing an independent kingdom! There was no lack of evidence against the "Long Fin," as it seems he was called in the secret records of the plot, and as he haughtily refused to plead any excuse, or even to give any account of himself, he was promptly declared guilty, and sentenced to be hanged. He remained immovable, and declined to ask for mercy. For reasons which do not appear, the sentence was commuted to whipping at the stocks, and branding with the letter R (rebel), after which he was to be sent out of the country. The brutal punishment was duly inflicted; the condemned man was sent to New York, where he was kept for a whole year in the "Stadthouse" and then sold as a slave to Barbadoes! If he was an impostor, it must be admitted that he played his part with rare skill, and bore his fate with a fortitude and haughty indifference utterly at variance with the general character of such pretenders. If he was really what he claimed to be—what a strange chapter he added by his great crime and tragic fate to the history of a family already so famous in the world for its marvellous adventures and terrible misfortunes!

A greater mystery still shrouded for many years a fair and lovely lady, whose cruel sufferings and romantic wanderings have furnished the plot for many a novel, and caused more tears to be shed, and more sorrow to be endured, than countless cases of far greater hardship. It was in the month of June, 1759, all nature was ablaze with the splendor of a Southern summer, that had not yet consumed the rich verdure of the hill-sides, when the little garrison of Fort Toulouse, in Louisiana, was in a state of utmost excitement. The lilies of France were waving proudly in the morning breeze, the guns shone bright in the early sun, and the soldiers were gathering around the gate, looking unusually happy and full of solemn expectation, for they had donned their best uniforms and were expecting a lady! At some distance from the fort, and under the shade of vast-spreading live oaks, stood several groups of Indians, concealing their curiosity under the mask of stoic indifference. But even their impassiveness gave way, when suddenly one of the great guns boomed forth a welcome, awaking the echoes of forest and hill-side around, and followed by a discharge of small arms, while the delighted soldiers, released for once from the fetters of discipline, rushed down to the stream to gaze at the novel sight. There was their captain, a man of striking appearance and looking his best, thanks to the rich uniform he had donned for the occasion, and the excitement he felt in his heart. There was a woman, the first white woman that had ever been seen in the lonely forests, holding in her arms a beautiful child, dressed gorgeously in delicate tissues and costly laces, and there was, above all, a lady of wondrous beauty, stepping lightly out of the dingy boat and falling, weeping, into the captain's arms. The new-comers were received with a wonder akin to awe, and walked slowly up to the simple cabin prepared for their reception, while the soldiers followed in silent admiration, and the red men looked haughtily at the white squaw that received so much homage. For even they were struck by the profound respect and exquisite courtesy with which the commander listened to every word that fell from his companion's lips, and the ready deference with which her slightest wishes were obeyed. At last the door was closed upon the strange group, and busy were the tongues that now discussed the new arrivals.

The beautiful lady, they all knew, was their captain's wife, and the little infant their daughter. But who had she been before? Then a marvellous story was told, and no one was found bold enough to doubt or to contradict, although they listened with wonder and almost trembled with vivid excitement, as the tale was unfolded. A fair German princess, Charlotte Christina Sophia, it was said, had been forced to marry the son of Peter the Great, Czar of all the Russias. She was the daughter of one of the many petty potentates who then abounded in the Holy Empire, and poverty and ambition had combined to hand her over to the Czarowitch Alexis, the future Emperor, although she and all the world knew him to be a man of fierce, uncontrollable temper, who little cared to conceal, under a thin, transparent varnish of refinement, the innate brutality of his race and his nature. The poor princess had to pay a fearful penalty for the apparent greatness of her position; it was all splendor and glory without, and fearful misery, unbearable wretchedness within. While high and low fell upon their knees, and in abject humility lay at her feet whenever she appeared in public, she no sooner returned to her home than she was made thus to kneel before her own master, who beat and ill-treated her, like a true savage. In vain did she bear all with angelic sweetness; in vain did her brother-in-law, the German Emperor, intercede in her behalf; in vain did even the mighty Czar, all-powerful in his realm, reprove his son— she was only made to suffer the more from the ill-will of her husband. At last the measure was filled to overflowing. She was on the point of giving birth to an heir to the crown, when brutal blows and drunken abuse destroyed the infant, and brought her to the gates of the grave. It was while lying thus sick unto death, that kind friends and faithful servants devised a plan for her to escape from the terrible fate that seemed to await her without hope of deliverance. Physicians and attendants, priests and friends, all united in reporting her gradual but steady decline, and when at last her death was announced, no surprise was felt, and all Russia mourned and grieved for the loss of one whom they had learnt to love and to prize. Thanks to the devotion of all who had ever come in contact with the fair princess, her lying in state, her solemn funeral and the final entombment, were all gone through with in perfect order and without the slightest suspicion. And yet she had never died! For as soon as the physicians had declared her case hopeless, and refused admittance to any one, Aurora Königsmark, the famous beauty, the friend of the King of Poland, had her quietly removed from the palace and concealed in the house of one of her German friends. When the funeral was over, and the excitement had somewhat subsided, she escaped from Russia under the protection of an old officer of her father's guard, and with him she landed on March 21, 1721, in Louisiana, passing unnoticed among the large number of German emigrants, whom the French financier, John Law, was then sending to his proposed colony in Arkansas. She lived for some years in Mobile, in quiet retirement, apparently the daughter of the white-haired old gentleman with whom she had arrived, and secluding herself rigorously from society, on the plea of her modest circumstances. But one fine day, as she walked thoughtfully along the shore, she came suddenly against a young French officer, who started as he beheld her, and could by no effort of his suppress the intense excitement her sight had caused in his heart. From henceforth she met him everywhere, timidly watching her steps and gazing at her from afar with wondering, amazed eyes. At last he found means to be admitted to her house and soon disclosed to her the fact that he had often seen her at St. Petersburg, when attached to the French embassador's suite, and that he had recognized her instantly at their first meeting. By a cunning stratagem he succeeded in throwing her companion off his guard and at last she confessed her great secret. It need hardly be added that such confidence soon grew into love, and that, when the fictitious father died, and left her unprotected, she could no longer resist her admirer's urgent prayers, and became the wife of the Chevalier d'Aubant. Thus, at least, he is called by Bossu, but Frederick the Great, who at one time became interested in the fate of the unfortunate princess, speaks of him as Waldeck. For ten years they lived in the distant colony, enjoying such happiness as probably all the splendor of a great court and the prestige of an Emperor's consort could not have afforded her, and when d'Aubant was sent to the distant fort, his faithful wife followed him to share his exile and to cheer his lonely life. Tradition has it that she loved to visit the poor Indians in their wigwams, to caress their children and to read to them the word of God, as far as she could make herself understood. To this day a solitary chimney, built of rough stones, and standing in a desolate, treeless wilderness, is pointed out as the site of her dwelling, and many are the wanderers from distant lands who visit the little town of Wetumpka (Ala.), in order to see with their own eyes the place, about three miles westward, where the great Czarowitch's wife lived so long amid French soldiers and savage Indians.

When her husband's health began to fail and to defy the skill of Colonial practitioners, she left with him the scene of her happiness, accompanied him to France, and, upon his appointment as Major, to the island of Bourbon.

Unfortunately the charming romance did not even last through her lifetime. Having become a widow, she returned with her daughter to Paris, where she was once more recognized by the tones of her voice as she was walking in the garden of the Tuilleries. The famous Marshal Saxe overheard her as she was conversing with a friend; he drew near, examined her features for a moment and at once addressed her, hat in hand, as the princess he had known in his early days. She denied her identity, but not earnestly enough to be obeyed in her wish to be left unknown; and privately steps were taken to provide for her in accordance with her rank. For some unaccountable reason, however, she preferred returning to Wolfenbuttel, the land of her birth, and here at last vengeance overtook her. She was again recognized, but this time not as Princess Sophia of Wolfenbuttel, but as one of the women attached to her wardrobe, who in her youth had not only borne some resemblance to her mistress but also stood high in her confidence. Consideration for her age and her many misfortunes induced the ducal family to deal leniently with the poor widow; she was allowed a small pension, but ordered instantly to leave the country, and died, not long afterwards, in 1771, in great poverty, in Vitri, near Paris.

LOST TOWNS.

VI.

 S the memory of man is happily so constituted that in course of time it ceases to recall with distinctness the darker days of our life, and only reflects bright and happy events, thus converting us all more or less into "garrulous praisers of former days," so history also is prone to record only the triumphs of a nation and to leave its failures and its sorrows to be buried in oblivion. Our own annals, brief as they are, begin already to show the same tendency, based upon the vanity of nations, but turned by Providence into a great and precious blessing. How many Americans, for instance, recall with accuracy the nature of the Dark and Bloody Ground, so often mentioned in our early accounts, so fearfully suggestive of days of brutal cruelty and ineffable suffering. We all have read, some time or other, that there is a portion of the land once owned by Virginia and known to the Shawanee Indians, who dwelt there, as Kaintuck-ee (at the head of the river), which was called the Middle Ground, when John Finlay, in 1767, crossed it for the first time, and which afterwards obtained the more significative name of the Dark and Bloody Ground. But

few of us recall the fact that this ill-fated region was reeking with blood long before the white man ever beheld its glorious prairies and noble forests ; that the Indians had fought for its rich harvests and abundant hunting-grounds for many a generation, and that more than one tribe had utterly vanished from the land in the course of these struggles. Their descendants would come, year after year, long after fertile farms and great cities had sprung up on the ensanguined plains, to bring their simple offerings to the graves of their forefathers, choosing strange out-of-the-way paths for their journey, and fearfully shrinking from certain well-remembered mounds and darkling pools, where the spirits of the departed were said to hover forever. After that, however, came another act of the great tragedy, when the children of the soil turned with one accord against the intruders from the East, and forced the early settlers of Kentucky to fight desperately for their homes and their lives. During the whole long period from 1769 to Wayne's victory on the Maumee, in 1794, blood was shed here almost daily. Surrounded by an enemy far outnumbering them, animated by deadly hatred and ferocious cruelty, wielding the same rifle with the whites, and as skilful in its use, these brave pioneers took, nevertheless, posssesion of the land, felled forests, laid out roads, built towns, and changed the wilderness into a garden. It is difficult to measure the greatness of their courage, more difficult still to fathom the depth and the weight of that darkness in which they worked undaunted and undismayed. For nearly twenty-five years a cloud of bloodthirsty Indians was forever hanging around them and darkening every bright moment of their life. No man could open his cabin door in the morning without danger of receiving a rifle bullet from a lurking enemy; no woman could go out to milk her cow without the risk of feeling the deadly scalping knife on her forehead before she returned. Many a man came home from his hunt to find a smoking ruin where he had left a happy home, or an empty hearth where wife and children had gladdened his heart; and gratefully he blessed God, if he found their remains and was thus spared the anguish of knowing them to be in the hands of incensed brutes.

Fortunately the work went on bravely and steadily; more and more fearless adventurers came from Virginia. James Harrod built, in the Spring of 1774, the first log house ever raised for family use in the new territory; famous Daniel Boone founded, in 1775, Boonesborough, on what he called Cantuck or Otter Creek, and already, in 1778, the Legislature of Virginia could incorporate the town of Louisville, so called in honor of Louis XVI., who was then lending his aid to the United States. As the cabins multiplied, and towns and villages arose, the red men fell back to safer hunting-grounds in the West, and soon the prosperity of a new and vigorous State made men forget the horrors of the Dark and Bloody Ground of Kentucky.

The same process went on even more speedily in other parts of the Union, where similar scenes had led to the bestowal of like names. Thus in the upper part of Ohio, also, a mournful region was long known as the Slaughter House, since here, for many a returning season, the stern Iroquois had met and fought the relentless Massawomee, a confederacy of Indian tribes dwelling in the country that lies on the Upper Ohio. The struggle was fierce, and ended in the utter destruction of the weaker party, but only after the soil had been inundated with blood, so that the Indians themselves had come to call the Ohio the Bloody River, and the scene of the terrific conflict was known among European settlers as the Dark and Bloody Ground of Ohio. Nor are other States without their sad memorials of like disastrous calamities. New York points with long-cherished grief at her Mohawk Valley, where all around Fort Stanwix—now the city of Rome—the cruelty of man converted smiling fields and blooming orchards into scenes of unutterable woe and wickedness. It was now Sir William Johnson, the lord of the great domain, who incited his followers and his red allies to bloody deeds, and now Joseph Brandt, the Sachem of the Mohawks, a regularly commissioned captain in the British army, who fell with his infuriated savages upon the homes of peaceful settlers. But here also peace soon returned with healing in its wings, and the Dark and Bloody Ground of the Empire State is now unknown beyond its narrow limits, and mentioned only in the annals of the local historian. Time has not yet had an opportunity to apply its soothing powers in like manner to the Dark and Bloody Ground of Arkansas, where a vast mass of ruins, but half hid under the shade of huge forest trees still speaks eloquently of a terrible massacre. Here once stood Fort Mann, held by a strong, but careless garrison; in a dark, stormy night, an immense war party of Pawnees suddenly and silently appeared under its towering ramparts; they scaled the palisades, they found the guards asleep, and the morning sun rose upon a scene of unspeakable desolation. The murderers had fled silently and suddenly, as they had come, and within the fortifications all lay still and stark,—not a groan was uttered, not a cry was heard, and only staring eyes and scalped skulls cried for vengeance to heaven. When the news reached the nearest settlements a fearful panic seized upon all; they left the fatal region, and for years after the terrible slaughter people spoke only with bated breath of the Dark and Bloody Ground on the Arkansas River.

If in these and similar cases we turn with a feeling of great relief from the places which know their former names no more, the impression is very different with most of the lost towns of our land. The country is still so young that ruins impress us painfully, like promising children called home in their early bloom; ivy and kindly mosses have hardly had time yet to cover with their green mantle the ugly scars and ghastly wounds; and poetry and legend, unknown to our youthful nation, have not yet come to weave the gossamer veil of pleasing fancy around the dismantled tower and the mouldering church. Where all is life and action, where a great nation, full of vigor and irrepressible energy, is hastening forward in the very rapture of motion, a ruin looks like a crime, and an abandoned town like the work of mysterious, vengeful Fate. And yet there is no lack of places in our land that once were busy marts and important centres of colonial life, where people ate and drank, married and were given in marriage, without dreaming of the impending destruction, and fancied themselves as secure as the ill-fated people of ancient Babylon. If these cities and towns had counted their inhabitants by thousands instead of by hundreds, or if some great catastrophe had destroyed them in an instant, all the world would bewail their ruin, and their tragic fate would be sung by the poets of every age. But their modest size and scanty population did not hinder them from being, in the early times of our existence, of vital importance to our New World, as our brave men were none the less heroes because they fought in log cabins instead of defending a Troy or a Carthage, or because they battled on an inland lake instead of encountering fleets in mid ocean. The very fact that these lost towns arose in the wilderness, and that their rise and their fall was neither watched by admiring multitudes nor recorded by the Muse of History, but adds to the romance of their fate, and calls upon us to point them out to every patriot and every student of humanity, as worthy of being better known and more fully considered.

Lost towns must naturally be mainly looked for in the older parts of our Union, and thus we find the most striking instance among them all in the Mother of States. We approach the New World with the first discoverers, whom a formidable storm had driven into Chesapeake

Bay, and behold with them "a country," as Captain John Smith reported, "that may have the prerogative over the most pleasant places knowne, for large and pleasant navigable Rivers; heaven and earth never agreed better to frame a place for man's habitation." We ascend with them the noble river, called by the loyal sailors the King's River, in honor of their dread sovereign, and reach, after a pleasant sail of some fifty miles, a bold headland, where vessels might safely ride in six fathoms of water, and yet be moored to trees on the shore. Here the adventurers rested, and were so pleased with the beauty of the prospect, the richness of the black loam and the great convenience for shipping, that, in the bonny month of May, of the year 1607, they determined to build a town on the spot, and forthwith named it "James Towne, in honour of the king's most excellent Majestie." They spoke of the site as an island, for it was surrounded on all sides by water, the great river to the South, and a small creek in the rear, but after a while it became a peninsula by the filling up of the back country, till in quite recent times neglect and high floods have once more deepened the water courses inland, and the place is an island again, as when it was first chosen to hold the second town ever built on this continent. Towns, however, were of slow growth in Virginia, and for many a year the little fort, with the few log huts around it, had a sore struggle for mere existence. Now wily Indians would come and attempt to burn it to the ground in order to drive the irresistible invaders out of their land, and now treacherous colonists themselves would attempt its destruction for purposes of private revenge or iniquitous plunder. John Smith tried in vain to control the restless spirits of useless gentlemen, and the idle hands of worthless criminals, who formed the majority of early settlers, but thanks to his marvellous tact and great personal influence, a youthful princess, " the Emperour's dearest daughter," would appear, like a beneficent fairy, whenever treason was ripe and threatened ruin to the infant colony, or waste and recklessness had produced a famine, and starvation was near at hand with all its horrors. As new immigrants came to fill up the land, and ambitious men began to covet colonial honors, the little town grew apace in size and importance, till, in the year 1619, the first Assembly ever held in Virginia could be convened in " James Citty" by Sir George Yeardley, Governor of the Colony. But even then already the good people of Virginia began to show in their ancient town the striking difference in character and mode of life, which marks them as distinct from their Puritan neighbors at the North. In the early days of Boston, we learn from a quaint old author, the Maine Law was curiously but clearly foreshadowed by its watchful authorities. In the year 1638, when the city boasted as yet of only twenty or thirty houses and two inns, Josselyn visited it, and was struck by the following custom. "An officer," he says, "visits the inns when a stranger goes into them, and if he calls for more drink than the officer thinks in his judgment he can soberly bear away, he countermands it, and appoints the proportion, beyond which he cannot get a drop." (Voyages, p. 173.) Jamestown, on the contrary, is described by the attractive author of the Westover MSS. (p. 3), as being about the same time a place " where, like true Englishmen, they built a Church, that cost no more than fifty pounds, and a tavern that cost five hundred." In the meanwhile trials and tribulations of every kind had fallen upon the unfortunate place, and in 1622, after the terrible massacre, in which nearly every Englishman, who dwelt not within the few fortified places, had been butchered by the incensed Indians, the town was actually abandoned by the terrified colonists. They even proposed to burn their deserted houses, and embarked for their homeward journey; fortunately they were met, while yet in the river, by some English vessels that brought supplies and reinforcements, and thus Virginia was not forsaken, and Jamestown, for a time at least, was saved. But the place would not grow in spite of all the natural advantages it offered, and the tempting inducements that were held out by the authorities. As late as 1662 a special Act of the Assembly was passed "That a towne be built at James Citty, as being the most convenient place on James River." (Henning's Statutes, II. p. 172). The end, however, was drawing near. Not many years afterwards Bacon's rebellion broke out. The unlucky Governor, Sir William Berkeley, utterly unable to cope with the talented and energetic rebel, was besieged in his capital and forced to flee for his life. When Bacon marched into the town, he found nothing but empty houses; everything that could be useful to the insurgents had either been carried away or sunk in the river, and the disappointment of the men was as great as that of their leader. He determined at once that the place, which could not be retained by himself, since it was incapable of defence against regular approaches, should at least not be a harbor and refuge for his enemies. He explained his resolution to his enthusiastic followers, who approved it by loud shouts and joyous acclamations. Firebrands and combustibles of every kind were at once prepared ; Bacon himself set the example, his lieutenants, Lawrence and Drummond, did not hesitate to set fire to their own houses, by far the most valuable in the town, and in a few minutes the church, the State house and all the other buildings were wrapped in a sudden and general conflagration. Thus ended James City, henceforth under the more familiar name of Jamestown, to remain one of our Lost Towns. A ruined tower, half overgrown with ivy, a few memorial stones in the graveyard which surrounded the church, hid under a dense growth of weeds and wild shrubs, and a melancholy pile of bricks, where once a tall chimney rose, gathering round its ruddy fire the brave colonists as they rested from their day's weary work, and loved to recall the friends and the joys of their sweet homes across the waters—these are all that remains now of the ancient town, once so memorable in the history of our country. No trace is left of the grave of Bartholomew Gosnold, the fearless sailor, who first of all brought his little bark across the wide ocean to sail up a noble river into a New World, and who died here, a victim of the climate and incessant labor, upon which "he was honorably buried, having all the ordnance in the fort shot off, with many vollies of small arms." (Purchas, IV. 1690.) No trace of the gallant Smith, first so grievously ill-treated, then worshipped with blind idolatry by the Indians, and finally lost to sight in an unknown grave, who here had told night after night his marvellous adventures of romance, while cheering the faint, intimidating the traitors, and painfully building up the infant colony. No trace of the English vessels that had here discharged, in 1619, a cargo well calculated to ruin a rising country, and more honorable to Virginia in its defeated evil influences than her most illustrious assassins from abroad. For in that year there had been landed on the tiny wharf of the half-starved town one hundred dissolute persons sent over " at express command of His Majesty, delivered by his Marshall," to be sold as servants, and, as if this were not poison enough to vitiate the feeble new settlement, these criminals had been accompanied by a hundred so-called Virgins, " sent over at the instance of the Treasurer (of the Company) for the purpose of fixing to the soil the roving and inconstant spirits of the colonists !" No trace of Pocahontas, the "king's sweet little child," who had sported here in childish innocence, listening at times to the strange foreigners' fearful tales, and saving, at other times again and again, the enemies of her race, at the peril of her own life, from imminent death and dire starvation. Here she had heard—the first child of the soil to whom the glad tidings of salvation were brought—the sweet words of the minister, Mr. Hunt, of whom it is recorded that when his little church, the first in all Virginia, was burnt down, together with his house, and he lost his books and everything but the clothes he wore, " yet none ever saw him repine at his loss." Surely, there is no spot in all America more brilliantly illumined by the splendor of romance, more strikingly illustrated by daring deeds, or more thoroughly sanctified by heroic suffering, than this little borough on the River James, and yet a crumbling ruin, soon to be seen no more, is all that now marks the place of the Lost Town.

There is something indescribably ludicrous in the indefatigable efforts which were made by Virginia to build up towns ; for in vain were ample rewards offered to German workmen and Dutch laborers, who would assist in building houses and forming communities; in vain did noblemen abroad and governors in the colony promise large sums of money to persons disposed to live within the well-fortified places ; in vain did even the Assembly of the Colony, by Acts and Proclamations, endeavor to encourage " Cohabitation "—as it was then quaintly called. Virginians have ever preferred a country life to town life, and the multitude of rivers and creeks, which form a vast network over the country, gave them from the beginning such abundant and easy means of sending their produce to market, that the usual inducements for congregating in towns were here almost entirely wanting. The difficulty of the task seems, however, but to have stimulated its advocates and patrons to ever new exertions, and it is almost touching to notice the perseverance with which effort after effort was made—and made in vain.

One of the earliest enterprises of this kind dates back as far as the year 1611, when Sir Thomas Dale was appointed High Marshal of Virginia and immediately took measures to carry out his favorite project, the building of a town. The Governor, Sir Thomas Gates, was quite willing to encourage his plans, and furnished him, in his official capacity, with three hundred and fifty chosen men, the majority of whom were German workmen. With this motley crowd the Marshal sailed up the King's River, exploring turn after turn, and discovering everywhere new beauties and new wealth, till he finally reached, in the month of August, the place where the impetuous stream falls over a number of rocky ledges, and navigation is at an end. Dropping down again some little distance he chose a place on what was afterwards called Taerar's Island, from the name of the man who bought it after the fearful massacre of 1622, and where the river makes the so-called Great Bend, performing a circuit of nearly seven miles, while the neck of land thus encircled is but a hundred and twenty yards across. It is one of the most curious features in the history of Virginia, and yet characteristic of many of her best enterprises, that here, at that remote time, a work was begun which was completed only in our own day. For these German settlers were, not long afterwards, employed to cut through this neck of land, for the purpose of straightening the course of the river, and thus shortening navigation. They were not allowed, however, to complete the work, which became popularly known as the Dutch Gap, so that it was left to a certain General Butler to continue the effort during the civil war, and to the impoverished State of Virginia to accomplish at last, in 1871, the work begun so long ago. It was near this place that Sir Thomas Dale determined to build his town, and he set to work at once, with his usual energy. " His new towne, within ten or twelve daies he had invironed it with a pale, and in honor of our noble Prince Henry, called it Henriopolis," says the chronicler of those days. The "pale" was a palisade, which ran from river to river, and formed a strong protection against the hostile Indians, and within its shelter there arose promptly a church and a storehouse. Gradually additions were made, till the place could boast of three streets of well-framed houses, while on the outskirts five forts, or watch-towers, had been erected, quaintly named Patience and Charity, Elizabeth and Mary, and Mount Malady, a "guest-house for sick people," on a high and dry place, with a beautiful view over the river and the surrounding landscape. Nor was the ministry forgotten, and Rock Hall, the spacious parsonage of the Rev. Mr. Whitaker, with its tall gables and ample glebe, spoke well for the esteem in which he and his office were held by the Marshal and his adherents. Friendly relations were established with the neighboring Indians, who soon learnt to appreciate the kindly feelings of the new master, and to dread his revenge whenever they attempted to injure his followers. As the town extended, its name contracted, and it became soon known as Henrico simply, but prospered so well, that when Sir Thomas Dale returned, in 1616, to England, Jamestown, Bermuda and Henrico constituted the whole of Virginia. A few years later efficient measures were taken to add increased importance to the place by making it the centre of all efforts in behalf of the conversion of the Indians. So well did the first settlers of the Old Dominion understand the peremptory duty that, following the noble example of Sir W. Raleigh, who, in 1588, had given £100 for the propagation of Christianity in Virginia, they ordered, in 1619, steps to be taken "for educating infidel children in the knowledge of the true God," and the sum of £1,500 was appropriated for the purpose, together with a tract of valuable land. The news of these proceedings seem to have created everywhere an enthusiastic interest in behalf of Henrico College, as it was first called, and when Sir Edwin Sandys obtained from the Company in England the magnificent gift of a hundred thousand acres, lying between Henrico and the present City of Richmond, it was insisted upon that it should at once be called the University of Henrico—a tendency to magnify a Grammar School into a University, not extinct even in our day. The main purpose of the new institution was to serve "as a College for the education of Indians," although it was also to "lay the foundation of a seminary of learning for the English." Contributions came in from all sides. The following year an unknown person sent five hundred pounds " for the maintenance of a convenient number of young Indians, from seven or under to twelve years of age, to be instructed in writing and the principles of the Christian religion, and then to be trained up in some lawful trade, with all gentleness and humanity, till they attained the age of twenty-one ; and after that, to have and enjoy the like liberties and privileges with the native English in Virginia." A Mr. Farrar likewise bequeathed a large sum, and twenty-four pounds annually, for the same purpose of "converting Infidel children;" and when afterwards an East India School was erected in the neighborhood, to be subject and preparatory to Henrico College for Indians exclusively, under the Rev. Mr. Copland, Chaplain to the East India Company, an unknown person sent a very large sum to the treasurer, signing himself with quaint humility, " Dust and Ashes." How nobly these acts and the accompanying sentiments contrast with the views entertained at a later period by the leading men of the same colony ! Now, all was tenderness and heartfelt interest in the earthly welfare and the eternal salvation of the poor natives, and due consideration was given to the claims of education and general enlightenment. Afterwards, Sir William Berkeley, whom high authority designates as "a worthy, good and just man," could soberly conclude his official report to the Lords of Commerce with these words : " I thank God there are no free schools, nor printing (in Virginia), and I hope we shall not have these hundred years. For learning has brought disobedience and heresy and sects into the world, and printing has divulged them and libels against the best government.

God keep us from both." Lord Effingham, Governor of Virginia in 1683, in the same spirit ordered to "allow no person to use a printing press on any occasion whatever," and Lord Howard of Effingham, who was Governor in 1684, actually taxed schoolmasters twenty shillings a head!

Superstitious people, who then saw the wrath of God in every public calamity, as they now see the workings of Providence in every accident by land or by water, failed not to ascribe the sudden and tragic end of all these efforts at "cohabitation," at enlightenment among the settlers, and conversion among the natives, to reasons closely resembling the views of the two governors. On that unfortunate day of sorrow, the 22d of March, 1622, every English life outside of Jamestown, and a few settlements nearer the coast, was taken by the Indians, and one vast massacre filled the colony with terror, and brought desolation to thousands of happy homes in England. Henrico was utterly destroyed, only a few fragments of the church, and of one house, remaining standing, and the whole country seemed to have received its death-blow. In the following year, Captain John Smith says: "So much scorned was the name of Virginia, some did chuse to be hanged ere they would goe thither, and they were." Town, school and university all have disappeared without leaving a trace of their former greatness behind them, and here, as in Jamestown, an ivy-mantled ruin is all that remains of the Lost Town.

Observant travellers have often been struck with the

beauty of the positions on which the early churches and convents of the Old World have been almost without exception erected. A similar instinct seems to have guided the first settlers in this country also, for nothing can surpass the magnificence of the view and the exquisite splendor of the landscape, afforded by places like Roanoke, in North Carolina, and Jamestown, in Virginia. The same attractions surround the most memorable Lost Town in the neighboring State of Maryland, where Leonard Calvert, in the month of February, 1634, wisely chose a site for the future capital of the Land of the Sanctuary. He had been sent over by his elder brother, Lord Baltamore, (for so the name was written in those days), the head of an ancient and noble house, originally from Flanders, and now the proprietor of a new grant of land, where he hoped to find larger rewards and greater comfort than in his bleak and barren dominion of Avalon, in Newfoundland. Sailing in the Ark and Dove—names suggestive of the peace among men it was proposed to establish in the New Colony—he had landed at Point Comfort, in Virginia, when he was, according to special instructions from home, received by the Governor with "courtesy and humanity," and had then sailed up the magnificent bay, known to the Indians as the Great Water or Mother of Waters (Chesapeake) and so called by Purchas (IV., 1646), while very old Spanish maps also designate it as Madre de Aguas. Soon the adventurers came to a place where the Potomac was over two miles broad, and a noble headland rose on the Northern bank, affording a magnificent view over the bay, and the smiling plains of the inland country. An Indian village crowned the point, called Yeocomoco, and here they were heartily welcomed by the natives, who hoped to find in the new-comers friendly allies in their struggle against the hostile Susquehannas. At the head of a river, called by Calvert St. George's River, and upon the highest table-land, the foundation was laid for the coming city. Father White, Calvert's Chaplain, assisted by his Jesuit brethren, planted his cross there, and said mass; then an imposing procession was formed, the litany of the cross chanted, and the ground solemnly christened with bell, book and candle. New names were bestowed upon land and water all around. The Heron Islands in the Potomac became St. Clement's, St. Catharine and St. Cecilia, and one of the bays, further inland, was dedicated to the Blessed Virgin Mary. The same name of St. Mary's was bestowed upon the town that was to be the capital of the new colony, and the thirty miles of territory immediately around the place, which had been faithfully purchased from the natives, received the name of Augusta Carolina, in honor of the reigning king, Charles I. As to the colony itself, a difficulty seems to have arisen here, strangely resembling the trouble which arose in connection with the naming of the neighboring province. There William Penn had been most anxious to secure to his magnificent purchase the title of New Wales, "being," as he said, "as this a pretty hilly country," and had employed humble petitions and direct appeals, nay, had even resorted to bribes, to accomplish his purpose, but all in vain. The king insisted upon calling it after Penn, the Admiral, and Pennsylvania, the "Holy Experiment," became in spite of the owner. So it was here, also, the Calverts wished to call the new country Crescentia, but Charles, in his charter, directed it to be called Terra Mariae, in honor of his queen, the daughter of Henry IV. of France, and thus it became Maryland. The pious priests were not indisposed to encourage a belief that the true sponsor was not an earthly sovereign, but the Queen of Heaven herself, and were, themselves, apt to call the colony the "Land of the Sanctuary," because it was the only home which religious liberty then had in the world.

The new town of St. Mary's soon rose to hopeful dimensions; a handsome church was erected, according to a design prepared by the great Inigo Jones himself; an imposing State House gave dignity to the capital, and comfortable dwelling-houses, built mostly of materials imported from the "home country," began to cluster around the stately buildings. Fort Point was thrown up on the right hand to protect the infant colony, and everything seemed to be prosperous and bright. An enthusiastic admirer of the new province, himself an early emigrant, J. Alsop, could write boastingly: "Let him look on Maryland with eyes admiring and he will then judge her The Miracle of His Age;" and add in another place: "Any one who desires to see the Landskip of the Creation drawn to the life, should see Mary-Land Nest in her green and fragrant mantle of spring." But slow, secret decay seems to have undermined the holy city from the beginning, though history is silent as to the true reasons for its speedy downfall. Without any apparent cause in climate or convenience, without any great public calamity, such as befell Jamestown, in the neighboring State, St. Mary's began to decline in spite of the lavish expenditure which the church and the pious proprietor seemed to be willing at all times to bestow upon their favorite city. In the year 1683 the seat of government, together with the courts and public offices, were ordered to be removed, and the poor town was doomed to an early death. The same mystery which envelops its fate seems to hang around the measures taken for the removal of the capital. There was evidently no fixed plan or purpose in the movement—the one thought of leaving St. Mary's being apparently the only well-known intention of all who were interested. So they went first to a wretched place, known as The Ridge, in a county called Ann Arundel, from Anna, the daughter of the Earl of Arundel, one of the most eminent among the Catholic peers of England, and the wife of Cecil Calvert, the second Lord Baltimore. From here the Legislature travelled to Battle Creek, on the Patuxent River, but finding the accommodations so insufficient that inns and school-houses had to be rented for the meetings of the Assembly, they once more returned to St. Mary's, and remained there till the year of the Protestant revolution. In 1692 the General Assembly met for the special purpose of recognizing the new sovereign, and at the same time made the Church of England the Church of Maryland, depriving the Catholics, the founders and faithful patrons of the colony of the right to hold office! With the supremacy of the old religion expired also the prestige of the old capital. The seat of government was now permanently transferred to a point of land at the mouth of the Severn, which was known as the Town Land of Severn, though popularly called Proctor's, from the name of the owner. In 1694 the place was made a port of entry, with a naval officer and a collector of customs, and received first the name of Ann Arundel Town, and later (in 1703) of Annapolis, in honor of Queen Anne. For a time the fatality that had so seriously injured St. Mary's seems to have pursued the new capital also, for even after many years of apparent prosperity, and in spite of ample grants and privileges, which had been bestowed upon the new favorite, it was in 1718 described as

> "A city situate on a plain
> Where scarce a house will keep out the rain;
> The buildings framed, with cypress rare,
> Resemble much our Southwark Fair—
> And if the truth I may report,
> It's not so large as Tottenham Court."
>
> (The Sotweed Factor, poem by G. Cook, Gent., 1711.)

In the meantime poor St. Mary's was speedily decaying; the public buildings were left unprotected, private houses were abandoned, and all went to wreck and ruin. From time to time spasmodic efforts were made to infuse new life into the dying town; but the very measures taken for the purpose bore in them the seed of failure: the bricks of the State House, erected for the special protection and benefit of Catholics, were used to build a Protestant church, the yard around was converted into a graveyard, and close to the former chapel a female seminary was established by means of a State lottery! No wonder, therefore, that St. Mary's also has disappeared, without leaving a trace of its former importance behind it, and belongs now to our Lost Towns, appealing to our sympathies by its melancholy fate and romantic interest. Like their favorite town the race of the Baltimores also has been extinct for a century, the last Lord of that name closing a sad life as a worn-out old man at forty, in Italy, and leaving no child by his wife Diana, daughter of the Duke of Buckingham. The Calverts also continued only through a natural son of the fifth Lord Baltimore; but the noble aspirations and liberal views of the ancient race have not become extinct in their descendants, nor have they been forgotten by those who admire pure virtue, and appreciate the rare merit of religious toleration.

Far down in the southernmost part of our early colonies there rises on the coast a vast mound, standing up solemn and solitary on the yellow sands, and looking like a weird beacon over the green sea before it and the beautiful country in the rear. Here, tradition says, a great Indian chief rests from his labors, who had on this spot met Sir Walter Raleigh, when he went on shore to explore the New World he had discovered. The Indian was so deeply impressed with the sweet gentleness and the grave dignity of the great sailor that he insisted upon being buried "where he had talked with that great, good man." So, at least, other Indians belonging to the sixth or seventh generation after the days of Raleigh, told another truly great and good man, as he stood on a fair spring morning near that memorable mound, and looked around upon the fair landscape, which he hoped soon to make a "home of the poor and the oppressed." Fifteen years before he reached these shores, that territory had already been granted by the "Palatine and Lords Proprietors of Carolina" to Sir Robert Montgomery, Bart., under the name of the Margravate of Azilia ; but no effort had been made to colonize the land, and there was an open field for the great benefactor in which to carry out the noble plan referred to by the poet of the Seasons in the lines

"O great design ! if executed well,
With patient care and wisdom—tempered zeal !"

The new owner was General Oglethorpe, who, in the year 1732, had obtained from the King the grant of a noble domain, lying between the Savannah and the Alatamahah Rivers, and intended to be held by him " in trust for the poor." He had been the leader of

—" the generous band
Who, touch'd with human woe, redressive search'd
Into the horrors of the gloomy gaol,
Unpitied and Unheard, where Misery moans,
Where Sickness pines, where Thirst and Hunger burn
And poor Misfortune feels the lash of Vice,"

and gathering around him a melancholy band of insolvent debtors, helpless orphans, and persecuted foreigners, he had embarked for the distant shores of the land which in honor of the monarch had been called Georgia Augusta. Here, on a noble river called Shewano by the Indians who dwelt on its banks, and who formed one of the twenty-eight tribes that were found in Carolina when the first whites settled on the Ashley, in a tent erected under the shelter of four beautiful pines, the old soldier had, on the first of February, 1733, begun to lay out the squares and streets of a noble city, and thus laid the foundation for the new commonwealth of Georgia. He was aided in his great work by strange friends and neighbors. Guided in his voyage across the ocean and in his first wanderings along the coast of the new province by the manuscript Journal of Sir W. Raleigh, he had now by his side the chief of the most recent colonies of the New World, Colonel Bull, of Carolina ; at another time George Whitfield, the gifted preacher, was his secretary and zealous assistant, while Attakulla-kulla, the Great Conjuror, a noble Cherokee Sachem, who had been to England, aided him in his intercourse with the natives.

As the new colony expanded, new settlements were made, and among these he loved best the town of his choice, on St. Simon's Island, where a little cottage, a garden, and an orchard of oranges, figs and grapes, of about fifty acres, formed the homestead of the illustrious founder of a State, and constituted all the property he ever owned on this continent. On a high bluff commanding the mouth of the river Alatamahah, which here swells out into a large bay, Oglethorpe built in 1736, a fort with four regular bastions, and mounted guns ; and under the shelter of this fastness nestled soon a thriving town, which he called Frederica, in honor of the eldest son of George II. This was the same unfortunate prince who died before his father, after giving his name also to the city of Fredericksburg, and to Frederick County in Virginia. The new town, according to the general's peculiar views already shown in the plan of Savannah, was regularly laid out; but the houses were either palmetto-cabins, mere "bowers and tents," as he loved to call them, or built of tabby, a composition of oyster-shells and lime. The little hamlet grew apace, until it could count more than a thousand inhabitants, and was full of life and commerce. The importation of rum and the holding of slaves had both been prohibited by the original charter, but vessels came soon to the safe harbor with commodities of all kinds; they also brought new settlers, now a band of Protestant refugees from Salzburg, who went up to their town of Ebenezer, and now Gaelic mountaineers, who built New Inverness, a genuine Castle Dangerous, on the Spanish frontier, "where wild Altama murmured to their woe." Here the delighted old soldier loved to sit and watch the growth of his colony, and from hence he sailed up the river to the dark forests, filled with Indians, or down the bay to the places on the sea-shore, described as "covered with myrtle, peach trees, orange trees and vines, in the wild woods." He protected his favorite Frederica still further by outlying forts, like those on Amelia Sound, so called after the queen, "out of gratitude to the king," and on Cumberland Island, the naming of which was due to an Indian. For as the general stood on its virgin soil, and the question arose how it was to be christened, a tall, stalwart Indian by his side, Toonakowi, the nephew of the famous Torno-

Chichi, drew out a gold repeater, which the Duke of Cumberland had given him when he was in England. "The Duke," he said, "gave us this watch that we might know how time went; we will at all times remember him," and then with true, in-bred courtesy, proposed to General Oglethorpe to call the island after the duke, which was done on the instant. The same prince gave his name, after the battle of Culloden, to Cumberland County, the first county created in the colony.

A strange, sad fatality seems here also to have attached itself to the first efforts of the new colony. General Oglethorpe was not rewarded on earth for his noble and unselfish labors. He saw rum forced upon his plantations, and slavery introduced in spite of his earnest remonstrances; Whitfield's mission failed, his orphan house fell to ruins, and his character was seriously endangered. The towns were alike unfortunate: Savannah was moved from Yamacraw Bluff, where it had first been laid out, down the river to its present site ; Ebenezer, the new home of the Salzburgers, was abandoned by them for unexplained reasons, and ere the old warrior had completed his life of nearly a century, his own town of Frederica had ceased to exist. A few ruins, overgrown with hoary moss, and ivy, a tall painted post here and there, and a silver coin found at times by chance visitors to the spot, are all that now speak of the once prosperous, promising town. A poor little hamlet near by still bears the name, but Frederica itself is no more ; its time-honored name must be added to the list of our Lost Towns.

"Bright were the days at Merry Mount, when the May-pole was the banner-staff of that gay colony," says Hawthorne, in one of his admirable Twice-Told Tales, and then goes on, weaving a few historic threads into a brilliant tissue of sparkling fancies, darkened and torn to shreds finally, after his manner, by the black shadows of some of his ancestors. Most readers follow him willingly —as who would not—in his bright fanciful wanderings, little suspecting that they read, after all, but a page from the grave annals of New England. For the gay crowd of merry-makers around the May-pole of Merry Mount consisted not merely of children of the poet's creative fancy: they really lived and revelled in reckless dissipation at Mount Wollaston, called so after a parish of that name in Old England. The place seems to have been haunted by weird visions from time immemorial, for the Indians already knew it as Pasonagesite, and had strange, sad stories to tell of the Manitous which appeared there to fanatic medicine-men and credulous maidens. Nor was the charm broken by the stern faith of the first English settlers: for years fearful tales were recited at even, when the doors had been fastened; the sword lay ready for the quick hand, and old and young gathered around the ruddy glow of the fire. It had received a new name now, and in cautious whispers and careful words Ma-re Mountain in New Canaan was spoken of as the place of the abomination of desolation. But the horror grew and the wrath increased when Morton, the reckless Englishman, formed a settlement on the ill-reputed place, and dared call it his "cheery towne of Merry Mount." He had gathered a motley crowd around him of broken-down gentlemen, tramps and vagabonds, idle and pleasure-loving apprentices, in fact all who could not endure the stern discipline and unbearable monotony of Puritan life. How they supported themselves, and how they supplied their wants not only, but their luxuries even, has remained a mystery to this day ; but there they were, rollicking, rioting fellows, who boasted that they were reviving and keeping up the ancient revels " in a solemne manner and merriment after the olde English custome." They continued their dancing and drinking, enjoyed their May-poles and merry games till the patience of the " Seperatists," as they are called by the chroniclers of those days, was exhausted, and they went forth, in holy wrath, to drive these sons of Belial from their mountain fastness. The terrible Endicott himself, who cut out the cross of St. George from the royal standard, and forced women to appear veiled in public assemblies, who smote the Pequots hip and thigh, and caused four Quakers to be put to death for their " abominable trembling and quaking," marched at the head of a troop of armed men against the forsaken sinners. The revellers were disgracefully defeated, and sent to the Puritans May-pole, the whipping-post; Morton, the leader, was loaded with chains and dispatched to England, there to stand his trial, and the poor town of Merry Mount destroyed, a lost town in the annals of America, and lost, alas ! also in eternity, according to the terrible views of its captors.

LOST LANDS.

VII.

THE traveller through Somerset County in England, sees, if he is coming from Bath, and faces the setting sun, the glowing light suddenly shut out from his vision by a strange, solitary eminence, which rises abruptly from low flats and monotonous marshes.   On the summit he beholds, clearly defined against the Western sky, tall spires, square towers, and grand old ruins with ragged outlines by the side of massive buildings, and lofty, oddly-shaped roofs. The whole looks as if it had once been enclosed by a high wall, and under the shelter of ancient convent and church, nestles a sleepy old town. He recognizes one of the great homes of miracles for which Great Britain was famous in olden days, and will not fail to look for the far-famed chapel which Joseph of Arimathea built here for the Britons, whom his zeal and supernatural power had promptly converted. But he may not recall that ancient Glassenbury, as Oldmixon spelt it in 1740, now Glastonbury, was still better known among our forefathers as Avalon, the Sacred Island. In ancient days that name had been given to the

Island of the Blessed, well-known to Celtic mythology, and dear to all lovers of fairy-land, for there was the true home of the fairies. How it was subsequently transferred to Glastonbury, an island only so far as it lies amid marshes and in the embrace of the river Brue, we know not, but its sanctity was early established and long maintained. The miraculous thorn of St. Joseph, which bloomed every Christmas day, the shrine of St. Dunstan, and the tomb of King Arthur, combined with a health-giving spring of supernatural power to keep up the charm and to attract every year ten thousands of pious visitors, who sought relief from disease, assistance from saints, or peace to troubled consciences at the holy shrines of old Avalon.

The word seemed to have a magic charm for all nations and all ages, for centuries after the great abbey had been built at Glastonbury, in 605, on the ruins of a British church, we find that Avalon had become the name of an island in the great ocean, "not far on this side of the terrestial paradise." In the centre stood a stately castle with a quaint treasure—a loadstone of irresistible power, which straightways drew all that came within its reach into the charmed circle. Here dwelt King Arthur and the great Oberon with Morgue la Faye, as all may read who love old French romances like Ogier le Danois, which contains a minute description of the enchanted island.

For the first time in the history of the Old World, a fairy tale was turned into a reality, and a land that had so long existed only in the fancy of pious enthusiasts or inspired poets was actually located on an Orbis Pictus, when, in 1628, Sir George Calvert, first Lord Baltimore, gave the name of Avalon—in grateful memory of Glastonbury—to a portion of our continent. Standing high in the favor of his sovereign, whom he had long and faithfully served in various posts of honor, he received upon retiring from public life, among other rich gifts, a grant of that part of Newfoundland which " lies between the Bay of Bulls on the coast thereof and the Cape St. Mary's on the South." This was erected into a province, of which he became sole proprietor, and here he proposed to establish an asylum for persecuted Catholics. Thus arose on our north-eastern coast the long forgotten Province of Avalon. He went to reside there himself, built mansions and cottages, established fisheries and farms, and lavishly spent his fortune in trying to make it a fit habitation for men, and a happy home for his fellow-believers. But the sterile, ice-bound land refused all return ; it seemed to be utterly unfit for cultivation, and after a few years' trial the owner turned his face towards the sunny South, and the world knew the short-lived Avalon no more. His successor, Cecil, nevertheless, kept the title, and his portrait appears with the inscription : *Effigies absoluti Domini Provinciarum Terrae Mariae et Avaloniae ;* but with him the title and the province both came to an end, and the latter is now, in American history, a forgotten land.

Was fabulous Avalon, which no doubt ceased to exist because fairies could not live amid perpetual snow and ice, the same as Norimbegua, the Meta Incognita of our forefathers? Who can tell? They have both had their day, when they formed the subject of courtly ambition and lordly grants, and they have both passed away, without leaving a trace on the maps of the world and in the memory of nations. The name Norimbegua occurs first, like Avalon, in connection with a purely imaginary country, lying somewhere between Nova Scotia on the North, and New England on the South. Here, it was believed, there dwelt once a strange nation of hoary antiquity, of weird appearance and awe-inspiring worship, who had built a great city, filled with inexhaustible treasures. Ogilby even speaks of the ruins of the city having been seen by bold sea-faring men of his time, who landed on the shores of the unknown country. Oldmixon—not always very reliable authority—speaks of "all the continent from South Virginia being, by the old Geographers, called Norim- begua," (America, I. p. 41), but applies the name, in his own account, to certain lands lying in New England, near Casco Bay. Gradually the strange word attracted the attention of learned men, and most subtle and ingenious explanations were given. Some contended for the Indian origin, and believed it to be the name borne by the ancient owners; others referred it back to the early Norwegian discoverers, who might easily have Latinized " Norge " into Norimbegua; while still others went so far as to suggest a colony of adventurous Germans from Nuremberg, who might in like manner have called the new country after their home in the fatherland. Purchas is the first to designate the locality more accurately by saying that "Pemptegoete is the place so famous under the name of Norimbega" (1632). This brings it once more close to New England, since "Pemptegeovett" is the first name given to the river Penobscot.

It is not a little curious that the mystery was by no means solved, but on the contrary made only deeper and darker, when the unknown land was solemnly erected into a grand vice-royalty, and generously bestowed upon a distinguished nobleman. This was in the days when brave Jacques Cartier's discovery of the St. Lawrence had filled the sea-faring world with wondrous tales of a river surpassing all the streams of Europe in grandeur, and watering a country as large and as beautiful as fair France herself. English and French adventurers of high rank and noble birth vied with each other in efforts to secure the enchanted regions of the New World for their own sovereigns, and France, especially, encouraged by her first great success on our Continent, was eager to beat her rival in the race. When, therefore, a bold and sagacious nobleman of Picardie, Francois de la Roque, Lord of Roberval, came from his province to the Court of Francis I., and petitioned for leave to visit the distant shores and to add new territories to his sovereign's realm, he was received with favor and warmly encouraged. By a commission, dated January 15, 1540, he was appointed Lord of "Norimbègue" and viceroy of all the immense territories contained within that mysterious province. (Charlevoix, Nouv. Tr. I. p. 113). No boundaries were prescribed, but no mention also was made of definite localities, save "the gulf and the banks of the river of St. Lawrence." Jacques Cartier was made the nobleman's Captain-general, and sailed with a fleet of five vessels a year before the new Viceroy. It was a motley crew he took with him to become citizens of Norimbega or Arambec, as it was frequently called; jail-birds for the greater part, and the very refuse of decaying inland towns and the slums of seaports. Nor were Roberval's followers apparently of better character; for he faithfully acknowledges that during the only winter he spent in the new province, one had to be hanged, and others "women as well as men" to be whipped. After a short twelvemonth's experience the mariner of St. Malo abandoned the enterprise; the Picard also remained but a year in his unpromising viceroyalty. He returned to France, preferring the modest competency of his castle in the province to the vice-royal splendor in his Northern dominion. Once more, however, his ambition was aroused, and placing himself at the head of a large number of adventurers, he sailed a second time for the New World. But if he did not share the fate of Verrazzani, who, we are told, "was the first to discover Canada, but for his sins, since the savages eat him" (La Hontan, Voy. I, p. 5), he was equally unfortunate. He was never heard of again, and the mystery that shrouds his end, fell like an impenetrable veil upon his province also. Norimbega disappeared with him from all records and charts, Hugo Grotius alone referring to it once more by the rather vague designation that it must have been situated "in Estotiland, because discovered by the Norwegians." Thus Norimbega also became one of our many forgotten lands.

It only shared, however, in the ungrateful treatment it thus received at the hands of men, the fate of previous and much older lands, which must have formed part at least of its territory. For it is well known that long before Frenchman or Englishman ever thought of crossing the Atlantic to explore the New World of the West, bold Northmen had already more than once sailed in their open boats through the stormy sea from Norway to Iceland and from Iceland to Greenland. Eric the Red, the first of their race who settled down in that portion of our Continent, had next sent his bold son, Leif the Lucky, with twenty-five well-chosen companions to the distant coast, and these had, in the year 1,000, fixed their abode there, building log-houses and tilling the ground. One of the men was a German, called Tyrker, and coming as he did from the vine-covered banks of the Rhine, he was struck with the grapes that ripened on every hillside and on many a lofty tree. So they called the new country Vinland, precisely as at a much later period other discoverers gave to the well-known island farther South the name it still bears: Martha's Vineyard. The Eastern portion of the Continent had, however, already been called Markland, or Wood Land, and continued to bear that name in the records of all discoverers till a late day. While it is surmised that these two names referred to the regions now forming Massachusetts and Rhode Island,

and the Island of Nantucket to the East, nothing certain is known about Vinland or Markland, and great is the zeal and violent are the polemics of the two parties, of which one stands up stoutly for the early discoverers and the importance of the two countries, while the other smiles skeptically at the accounts of Eric the Red, and Leif the Lucky, and denies that their new homes in America are forgotten lands—because they never existed!

The same mystery which thus concealed the Easternmost parts of our Continent for centuries from the eager eyes of Europe, seems for a time at least to have barred the way to an accurate knowledge of the Northwest. Here also a half-fabulous, half-mythical name, Ania, meets us, of which no accurate record is left, no explanation is given. All we know is, that on the very oldest maps of America the Northwestern part of the great continent is called Ania, and that the long-sought water-channel to the North of our land was hence known as the Anian Straits. It is one of the most interesting features of our early annals that they present to us an almost uninterrupted series of efforts to discover a way by water that should allow vessels to go directly from Europe to distant Cathay. Men of indomitable energy and full of confidence in final triumph started, ever and anon, from the first voyages of "John Kabotts, the Venician," in 1498, to the last days of Franklin and Bellot, to discover these fabulous Anian Straits. During all the time that lies between Gaspar Cortereal, the renowned Portuguese navigator, who in 1499 explored the coasts of Labrador, who claimed to have sailed through a narrow channel, westward from the Atlantic, into another great sea communicating with the Indian Ocean, and the sad hour when the brave French sailor paid with his life for the honor of having discovered an open passage, the shores of Northern seas have been lined with the bleaching bones of hapless searchers after these Anian Straits.

At last the hero came that was not only to discover the truth about these fabulous regions, but actually to become the first crowned king of a portion of our Continent. This was Sir Francis Drake, who had, from a cabin-boy, risen to become the pride of England, the founder of her naval greatness, and the terror of Spain; whose fleets he destroyed and whose commerce he ruined. Having seen, from a mountain top, at Darien, the placid waters of the Pacific, he determined to explore those seas, in which the flag of the Tudors had never yet appeared. He left England, on this great enterprise, in December, 1577, roved through the Atlantic, pillaged the Spanish possessions in Peru and Chili, and in early Spring of the following year reached the coasts of California. On the 17th of June, "after much buffeting, it pleased God to send him into a fair and good bay, within 38 degrees of the line," (probably the port of Bodega) and here he determined to rest and refit. During the next five weeks he succeeded in making such an impression upon the natives, that they came in crowds, and with all the powers of persuasion they possessed, and offering all the riches they thought might be tempting to the great stranger, besought him to remain as their king. Drake "thought not meet to reject the crown; thereupon, in the name, and to the use of her Majesty Queen Elizabeth, he took the crown, sceptre and dignity of the country in his own hands, wishing that the riches and treasures thereof might be so conveniently transported for the convenience of the kingdom at home." The scene must have been ludicrous in the extreme, and the naïve description of it in Sir F. Drake's voyage, by Francis Pretty (Hakluyt, 1589,) is full of interest and unconscious humor. There was the great captain in all the pomp and circumstance of a commander of those days, superbly equipped in English harbors, and enormously enriched by a royal galleon, laden with plate, which he had recently taken; around him his companions-in-arms, men of noble and gentle birth, and all the picturesque outfittings of an age that loved splendor and delighted in gorgeous colors. On the other side a tribe of naked savages, adorned only with the rude emblems of barbarous warfare, and decked with the teeth, the claws and the wings of birds and beasts, offering the barren sovereignty of a wretched coastland to a being revered as a powerful god. It is difficult to imagine how the great captain and his illustrious companions could have submitted with patient endurance to the strange ceremonies and uncouth worship of the wild Indians; nevertheless, the whole solemn pageant of a coronation was duly performed, and Drake, having assumed the dignity and title of Hioh—whatever that may have meant in California—bestowed upon his new kingdom the name of New Albion. Pillars were erected on the coast, emblazoned with the arms of Old England, and bearing high-sounding inscriptions, which proclaimed to the world the sovereignty of its Queen over these regions, and the rights then formally vested in the great naval commander.

Giving no heed to the fact that the Spaniards had many years before already discovered, and even partially occupied the coast of New California, he claimed by the act of discovery the right to name that vast and magnificently rich country, which in course of time will, no doubt, become New America, and make of the Pacific Ocean the Mediterranean of a coming age. In vain did the Spaniards loudly protest; in vain did cautious writers allude to previous records; New Albion it was and remained for several centuries. When Sir F. Drake, having failed to discover in his turn the long-sought open passage to the North of America, had sailed around the globe and received, a newly-made knight, the Queen as his guest, on board his ship in the harbor of Plymouth, he could proudly lay at her feet the crown of a kingdom on the Pacific, and greet her as the sovereign of New Albion. Can we wonder that the English clung to the name, in the face of all better rights, and despite the most vehement protestations? An order of the admiralty, dated June 6, 1776, and directing Cook to proceed to the coast of New Albion, which he was to reach in the latitude of 45 degrees, shows by the application of that name to the north-western coast of America, that Great Britain had no intention yet to give up her rights to the region which she claimed to have been acquired by Drake nearly two hundred years before. It is true that the name, though not yet disused, had in the meantime fallen back into the realms of myth: the distant unknown region, utterly cut off from all intercourse with England, had long since faded away into the dim distance, and had thus become the favorite scene of extraordinary adventures and Utopian romances. Bacon placed there his Utopia, and Brobdignag, if we rely on the statements of that veracious discoverer, Captain Lemuel Gulliver, must have been in New Albion.

The romantic country is now a forgotten land; in its place have arisen Oregon, recalling by its melodious name the Origans or sweet marjoram that grows on the banks of the great river of the West (Darby's Gazetteer), and Washington, ready to transmit to the Pacific empire the name of America's greatest son.

As there are few great revolutions in history that have not had their mimic counterpart in some tempest in a teapot, and few great names without their burlesque echo in low life, so New Albion, also, has had its caricature and mocking counterfeit in the annals of our early days. Brave Captain John Smith, trying to describe in his uncouth, but surprisingly accurate manner, the lands of the new continent, and especially of the regions of New England, which owe to him their name and their existence, says quaintly: " New England is opposite to Nova Albyon, in the South Sea. New France, off it, is Northward, Southwardes is Virginia, and all the adjoining countries, with New Granada, New Spain, New Andalusia, etc."—(a Description of New England, 1616). Little did he imagine, at that day, that another New Albion—not on the South Sea—would, ere long, come and claim, not only the privileges of a neighbor, but even the right of ownership to part of his beloved Virginia. And yet, it was only in 1648 that a pamphlet appeared, entitled : "A Description of the Province of New Albion, in North America," which in its more modest introductory pages speaks of New Albion and New Scotland as parts of Virginia, and in other places, more unreservedly claims nothing less than "all America" for the new province. The ambitious author, bearing himself the high-sounding names of Beauchamp Plantagenet, with ineffable arrogance, transforms a simple and unpretending country squire, Sir Edmund Plowden, of Shropshire, in England, unto a high and mighty Earl Palatine, and a certain strip of land, being in possession of rightful owners, and under colonial government, into that Palatine's great "Province of New Albion." The claim appears at first sight so preposterous, and the existence of the magnificent domain is so entirely fictitious, that many careful writers have held the whole to be either a mere myth or a deliberate hoax. There can be, however, no doubt that the province once existed—at least upon parchment—for it is frequently mentioned in historical works, in Burke's History of the Commoners, etc., and at least referred to in Beverly's History of Virginia (I, p.

49). From these statements it would appear that Sir Edmund Plowden really received through the favor of his patron, the famous Lord Stafford, and in his name as Lord-Lieutenant of Ireland, a patent under the Great Seal, assigning to him certain lands in Northern Virginia, "sometimes called New Canaan," on the shores of Delaware Bay, and probably lying somewhere near the present town of Salem, in the State of New Jersey. To the grant was added the title of Earl Palatine, with all the rights and powers of creating provincial, feudal and local barons, knights, bachelors, etc., the whole to be held from King Charles I., " as of our crown of Ireland in capite." The patent, duly recorded, is dated June 21, 1634; but for many years no efforts seem to have been made to profit by its privileges, the Earl Palatine being apparently too poor to fit out a vessel for himself, and the distant province too uninviting to attract public enterprise. At last he sailed with a number of emigrants to his new province, but having neglected to provide himself with a pilot, he was unable to find the entrance to Delaware Bay, however wide open its magnificent waters may generally be to new-comers, and saw himself forced to land in Virginia. Here more misfortunes must have befallen him, for we are told in Winthrop's History of New England, that he "lost the estate he had brought over, and all his people scattered from him." The poor Earl Palatine *in partibus infidelium*, after seven years' painful waiting, made his way successfully to Boston, probably never once seeing his lordly domain, and there remained for some time, till a vessel took him back again to his hereditary acres in Shropshire. This melancholy failure, however, did not prevent his faithful follower, Mr. Beauchamp Plantagenet, from describing in his book, most minutely, the beauties and wonders of the new Palatinate, with all the noble seats of the princely owner, nor did he fail to enumerate the Lords and Barons whom his great chieftain had made by virtue of his patent—beginning with wise charity at home and bestowing most gorgeous titles and surnames upon all of his children, down to a noble baron, crying lustily in his cradle. And thus ended the Province of New Albion. The Swedes, who were mainly settled on the lands it embraced, were never dispossessed and probably never even heard of the attempted transfer of their allegiance. Virginia was already great enough to treat the "defalcation" of her territory, as it was then called, with contemptuous silence, and the new country, in fact, never had any existence at all except upon paper. A last faint echo of its early pretensions was heard in the year 1784, when a certain Charles Varlo came over from England, and, claiming to act as representative of the "Earl of Albion," threatened to institute legal proceedings against all "trespassers upon the province." Philadelphia lawyers, formidable to English authorities, from the days of Andrew Hamilton's pleadings in Leisler's case, must have appeared too threatening to him, since nothing more was heard of agent or principal, and New Albion, of the Atlantic, also, may fairly be considered as one of our lost lands.

The peaceful settlers whom the ambitious Earl Palatine was so anxious to dispossess of their modest homes were, however, only spared for a time. They might resist a single claimant, supported only by the portentous sound of a royal Patent; but they were hopelessly lost, when a nation's power was arrayed against them, and the question became one not of right but of might, and thus their efforts to create a New Sweden by the side of New England were rendered abortive.

As long ago as the year 1590 an eminent and enterprising merchant of the Netherlands, named William Ussellinx, had conceived the idea of a West India Company, which was to acquire lands, establish towns, and profit by active trade on our Continent. He had been a great traveller in his day, living some years in Portugal, Castile and the Azores, and ever watchful of commercial openings, had shrewdly observed the course of trade. But in those days the dangers of such an undertaking were still too appalling, and he did not succeed in his native land. Leaving Amsterdam in a passion, he found himself, in the course of his wanderings, in distant Sweden, and like all men of large views and liberal impulses, was filled with great and sincere admiration for the noblest of Sweden's Kings, Gustavus Adolphus. To him, therefore, he addressed himself with his favorite scheme, cherished in his heart and never abandoned for full thirty years, and fortunately, he obtained not only a hearing, but found a willing listener. Those were days when all Europe was filled with a desire to share in the rich harvest of colonization, which had already added so much to the power and the prestige of Spain, England and France; and the enthusiasm, with which such enterprises in a new world were then pursued, had gradually reached, also, the northernmost regions of Europe. There was another motive, however, in the heart of the pious king; he was already preparing to abandon his throne, the land of his fathers, and all that was dear to him upon earth, in order to prove, with his life's blood, his devotion to religious liberty, and thus he was naturally led to look beyond the great sea for a home, where persecuted brethren might find a shelter, and the weary be at rest. He promptly ordered, therefore, an examination of the proposal, and as there was found a tract of land lying between the colony of Virginia and New England, to which no European power had as yet laid any claim, he determined to take possession, and to found there a new and free Sweden. A charter was promptly drawn up and signed, but unfortunately the king's affairs had become, in the meantime, so pressing, and the Polish war now engaged his attention so closely, that nothing more was done at that time. Usselinx, however, who had waited well-nigh a lifetime, could afford to be patient, and at last his perseverance was rewarded. The king had, only a few days before his tragic death on the battlefield of Lutzen, recommended the scheme to his wise chancellor Oxenstiern, as "the jewel of his kingdom," and the latter found time, while commanding the armies in Germany, controlling the cabinets of Europe, and ruling a kingdom at home, to attend to the humble merchant and his far-seeing plans. Great was the joy of the good people of Stockholm, when, on a bright autumn day, in 1637, the two stout vessels, Griffin and Key of Kalmar, left the rock-bound harbor amid loud shouts and devout prayers, while from all the heights resounded joyous shouts, and the bells were ringing merrily from church and chapel. But greater still was, no doubt, the silent joy of the gray-haired man on deck of the Griffin, who saw, at last, the wish of his life on the point of being realized, and felt his heart glow with delight at the idea of founding a new empire on distant shores.

"The consequences of this design," the great chancellor had said, when extending the charter to Germany, "will be favorable to all Christendom, to Europe, to the whole world." And he, Usselinx, was the chosen instrument of Providence, to carry out this great enterprise. But by his side stood another Dutchman, very different in character, and actuated by motives of purely personal interest. This was Peter Minnits, once pompously styling himself Governor of New Netherlands, but in reality nothing more than an humble factor of the East India Company for their trade with the Indians, and the transmission of beaver skins to their store-houses in Holland. In the strife of factions, and probably from want of capacity, he had lost his place and had been expelled from the colony. Hearing in Germany of the proposed expedition, he had promptly hastened to Sweden, and with ineffable impudence offered himself as a guide and an agent to the new company, though fully aware of their purpose to occupy the land and appropriate the trade, which his countrymen claimed as their own, and which he had once been sent to protect as their governor. The two ships, taking the Southern passage, did not reach our shores till early in the following year, and there is something indescribably touching in the enthusiasm with which these simple children of the North, reduced by a long, tedious voyage, greeted the first sight of land. In their delight they called Cape Inlopen, the interior Cape of Delaware Bay, Paradise Point, and with great joyousness landed on the banks of the mighty river. The little company of Swedes and Fins adopted, at once, the policy prescribed by their pious king, and their wise minister, which has marked them among all the colonists that have ever come to this land; they bought all the lands they wanted from the Indians, paying scrupulously for them, now with a piece of baize and now with a keg of nails, always drawing up a paper to be signed by the natives with a beaver or a mountain, a bow or an arrow, as their token might be; and they refused to have slaves, "for," their first charter said, "the Swedish nation is laborious and intelligent, and surely we shall gain more by a free people with wives and children." Finding the land unoccupied, and buying it for a fair price from the rightful owners, they defied the protests of their Dutch neighbors; besides, the name of Sweden stood high in those days, and her children were respected and feared wherever they appeared.

So they settled in what is now Delaware, from the South Cape to the falls of the river near Trenton, and built a Fort, which they named Christiana, from "the sweet little jasmine-bud in the royal conservatory," the little girl who was then seated upon the throne. A Swedish architect, Peter Lindstrom, laid out a town; trade sprang up with the Lenné-Lenapés, an iron mill was erected after the manner they had learnt in their own rich mines at home, and God's blessing rested visibly upon the infant colony. More settlers came over from Sweden and Finland, allured by the reports of the loveliness of the New World, where food was abundant and poverty unknown; a second supply, under Governor Prints, reached the New Swede River in 1642, and " New Sweedland," as Holme calls it naively in his history (Stockholm, 1702), on the New Swede River, the Delaware, began to expand and to prosper. They had ere long another Gottenburg and Elsinburg to remind them of their homes in Sweden, and the Norwegians among them built a new Bergen. Moreover, they soon became quite famous in Europe as well as in the New World, as the only people to whom the *Odium Theologicum* was unknown. Catholic and Protestant, Puritan and Cavalier were all treated with the same simple cordiality, and welcomed if they came to settle among the Swedes. But of all the forlorn and persecuted believers of that day none more gratefully acknowledged this truly Christian practice than the poor Quakers, who in those days bid fair to rival the Jews in their homeless condition and sad sufferings. In Massachusetts the mere fact of belonging to "the cursed sect of heretics" exposed them to the penalty of being immediately sent to the House of Correction, to be whipped with twenty stripes, and to be kept at hard labor till they could be transported. Pious Cotton Mather added the privilege of having their heads shaved, and of being compelled to attend congregational meetings under the penalty of "five shillings for each offence." In Maryland, according to an ordinance passed as late as the year 1661, they might be apprehended and whipped by any justice of the peace. Virginia characteristically punished them with a fine of 5,000 lbs. of tobacco, while New York threatened immediate "imprisonment and flagellation." Among the Swedes only were the poor Friends sure of being not only tolerated, but cordially received and hospitably entertained.

Thus New Sweden became so important, thanks to the great name Sweden then enjoyed throughout the world, and thanks to the rapid increase of the colony itself, that at one time it actually threatened to overshadow its two great competitors for colonial greatness. So it would at least appear from the remarkable statement we find in an old French writer, who adds to his description of New France the words: "To the South West lies Virginia, which jointly with New Holland was formerly known by the name of New Sweden!" (L. Hennepin, Nouv. Découv, II. p. 170.)

This great and unexpected success soon excited envy and bitter enmity; besides, the infant colony was dangerously hemmed in between two powerful neighbors—the English in Virginia to the South, and the Dutch of New Amsterdam to the North, to say nothing of the boisterous claims of New Albion and the threatening plans of the great Quaker. When the struggle came, there was little doubt as to the end. The Dutch, most deeply interested in the trade of the "tobacco of Virginia and the beaver skins of the Schuylkill," and irritated by the quiet but active industry of the new settlers, determined to drive them out and thus to rid themselves of formidable rivals.

The struggle was brief and bloodless; but a sad disappointment to the Swedish people at home, who thus saw the only Colony they had ever planted destroyed at a single blow, and a great grief to the Swedish settlers, who had lived in happy peace with all their neighbors and were little prepared for the storm that swept over them. It was but a year after the first Swedish deed drawn up in Stockholm had been read once more, for confirmation, to a large assembly of Indians at Tinicum, a fort on an island in the river near Philadelphia, in which New Swedeland's boundary lines were carefully explained. The good people of the Colony had been deeply touched by the strong emotions which the Indians had shown in face and gesture, as the names of the original signers were mentioned one by one—now brightening up and uttering low sounds of delight as the living were called, and now bowing their heads in mute sorrow, as the reading recalled the memory of the departed.

For not even William Penn's Friends ever lived with the natives in fuller sympathy or closer brotherhood. A little army of six hundred men from "below Breucklen," under famous Old Silverleg, as Governor Stuyvesant was frequently called, came sailing up the broad Delaware bent upon conquest. This was in September, 1655, and before the month had ended, every Swedish fort had surrendered without an attempt at resistance, and there was an end of New Sweden.

If the colony which connects our New World with the icy regions of Scandinavia is one of our lost lands, the Swedes themselves have yet left their mark almost indelibly behind them. A number, it is true, unwilling to live under their new and unpopular masters, went back to their native land, but many also took the oath of allegiance to the States-General and remained fondly clinging to their speech and their faith. As late as 1749, Kalm, the great botanist, found Rapaapo inhabited by Swedes only, not a single Englishman or foreigner living among them, so that they had preserved their vernacular unchanged and unmixed (Travels II. p. 28). Nor ought it to be forgotten that the great proprietor of Pennsylvania actually purchased the site of his city of Brotherly Love from these Swedish brothers, called Soen's Soener, whom he found it a difficult task to move from their simple, but endeared homes. There were no less than three Swedish churches there when Penn first came to his new province (Proud's Pa., I. p. 204), and one of these, a wretched old building, standing in one of the suburbs of Philadelphia, was religiously preserved for a hundred years later, as a memorial of the happy days of New Sweden.

It is but natural to ask, who were these proud six hundred, who under their commander Stuy, as he is contemptuously called by the English captain to whom he succumbed in turn, who thus came and with the strong hand, in the face of law and of justice, destroyed a fair colony, and added one more to the list of lost lands? They were the men of a sister colony, which only a few years later was to fall by the sword even as they had conquered the poor handful of Swedes with the sword. For New Netherlands, also, a great and powerful province, the dread of New England and the terror of the Indians, was soon to be stricken from the roll of our colonies and to be forgotten after a few generations. There is a melancholy interest in the utter oblivion which had fallen upon the early Dutch days, eclipsed as they were by the vast energy and rapid increase of the English rule that followed their quiet happiness. We all know how the bold Italian sailor, John Verrazzani, under orders from Francis I., set out with a single caravel to discover new lands and earn new fame. His brave little vessel, the Dolphin, having "the good hap of a fortunate name," carried him safely across the wide ocean, and in March, 1524, brought him, the first European, to the islands that border the shores of North Carolina. Thence he sailed up and down our coast, and in the course of his wanderings entered a noble harbor, anchored there to make soundings, noticed its vast size and great safety, and after casting covetous eyes at what appeared to be silver in the hillsides of New Jersey, and giving the natives the first taste of their future curse, Aquavitae, sailed away again, leaving the magnificent bay to an undisturbed rest of nearly eighty years. No name has been handed down to us belonging to this early voyage (Hakluyt III. 360) save one, the oldest of all American names, and full of sweet memories of the beautiful mother of King Francis. Verrazzani bestowed upon an island, reminding him of Rhodes, but now known as Block-Island, the name of Louise. We all know, in like manner, how Henry Hudson, abandoned by the English, and having made two voyages in vain, though battling manfully against the icepacks off the North Cape, had entered the service of the Dutch East India Company, and on the 25th of March, 1609, started boldly for the formidable regions of Nova Zembla; how, driven by fierce west winds to Newfoundland, he had sailed down as far as Charleston harbor, and then turning once more Northward, had, by sheer accident, discovered Delaware Bay; how, finally, on the 3rd of September, he had cast anchor "at two cables' length from shore," within Sandy Hook, and there "rode in five fathoms oosy ground, and saw many salmons and mullets and rays very great." But we are apt to forget that, as his discovery was the result of mere chance, so it also ended, as far as he was concerned, in utter failure. He sailed up in his famous Half Moon, following the windings of the noble river that still bears his name, full of hope that, at last, he had found the much-coveted Northwest passage, which was to give him access to Western seas and thus lead him straight to Cathay ; but, when he found the river growing smaller and the soundings more shallow, he returned with grief in his heart and bitterly disappointed. Fortunately there were shrewd and cunning men at home who foresaw the full value of the newly-discovered land, and soon more vessels were sent out and settlements were made at the mouth and on the banks of the river. When Hudson passed the noble gateway of the Narrows and thus first entered upon the waters of the magnificent stream, he heard it called Mahicannibuck by the Indians, a name meaning, River of the Mountains. On the next voyage the Dutch called it Mauritius, in honor of the Stadtholder of the Netherlands, Prince Maurice, who favored the new colony. A few years later, in 1614, Adrian Block, one of the boldest Dutch navigators of those days, when there was no lack of fearless sailors on every sea of our globe, had filled his good ship Tiger with bear skins and was about to return to Amsterdam, when a fire reduced his vessel to a wreck and forced him to seek shelter on land. The December snows had already fallen, and there was thick ice in all the coves. But he was not to be daunted, and encouraging his men by cheerful words and brave example, he soon succeeded in building a few rude log huts and a storehouse on Manhattan Island (Beaver Street recalls the place and the purpose), erected a fort in the centre, and there spent the winter—not in idleness though, for with his good men he built a new vessel, and before the

Spring blossoms appeared, his "Onrust" was ready to take him away. He never returned, but "Unrest" has ever since been a name well deserving of its early connection with the great city. Thus it was that when Sir Thomas Dales and Captain Argall came up from distant Virginia to look into the beautiful harbor, they could find there, "on Manhatas' Island, in Hudson's River, four houses built, and a pretended Dutch Governour, under the West India Company's of Amsterdam part or share." The name of Manhatas did not, however, then appear for the first time. An unknown author goes even so far as to ascribe it to the days when Verrazzani appeared there for the first time, and states that it meant the Place of Drink, in allusion to the Aqua Vitæ given to the natives. In Neal's New England the island is called Manhanatoes, while Burke speaks of Monadas as the "Indian name for the island whereon New York stands." (Va. II. p. 150.) A letter, written March 9, 1627, by the "Governour of the Dutch Plantation at Hudson's River," is dated "at the Manhattas in the Fort Amsterdam," and here, in 1656, the Dutch began their town of New Amsterdam (Proud, Pa. p. 110), which ere long was by its wise liberality and kind-hearted toleration to become equally obnoxious to Puritans, Churchmen and Romanists, "a cage of unclean birds," as it was contemptuously called—and sometimes is called even now for very dissimilar reasons.

The little colony, with its beautiful harbor below, and Fort Orange above, on the great river, soon grew and prospered till it became, in the enthusiastic words of one of the early settlers, " het schoonste land dat men met voeten betreden kan "—(the fairest land on which men can set foot). But if its growth was rapid, its life was short. With that supreme disregard of the rights of others, which is one of the most striking characteristics of the Stuarts, Charles II. bestowed, in 1664, the whole of what he was pleased to call Nova Belgia, on his brother, the Duke of York, and prompt measures were taken to obtain possession. In the quaint words of a contemporary writer: " Four commissioners were sent over, who, marching with 300 red cotes to the Manhadaes or Manhatoes, took from the Dutch their chief town, then called New Amsterdam, and on August 29 did turn out their Gouvernour Hardkoppig Piet (Hardheaded Peter) though he was, and all the rest but those who did acknowledge subjection to the King of England, suffering them to enjoy their houses and estates as before." (A Prospect of New York, London, 1685.) It is true that Dutch remained the prevailing language down to the days of the Revolution, and that Holland contrived to be the nursery of the colony long after the conquest by the English, but, nevertheless, as New York soon caused New Amsterdam no more to be remembered, New Netherlands also very speedily was eclipsed by the new State and may fairly be looked upon as one of our lost lands.

Nor are the Northern States, even steady New England, without their sad reminiscences of provinces that were carved out, and dominions that were projected only to leave a "name and nothing more" behind them. How few of us have ever heard of Muscongus, and yet the word has its important place in our history, and its most mournful tragedies besides, to touch our hearts. A great patent had been issued as early as the year 1629, concerning about a million of acres of land on the river Penobscot, with the river Muscongus on the south-west, "and extending ten leagues north-east of the Penobscot and ten leagues into the country." So large was this magnificent domain that it lay only partly within New England, while a portion extended into New France. It was known as the Waldo Patent, from the name of the proprietor, and as Muscongus, from the river on which it was mainly situated. When Charles II. created the province of Maine in favor of his brother, the Duke of York, the whole domain was absorbed in the new grant, but remained well known till the Revolution as Sagadahock. At a later period an effort was made to revive the patent; a joint-stock company was formed to have it surveyed, and to induce settlers to take possession; but it was almost an unbroken wilderness, and only a few hundred Germans could be tempted, in 1739, to settle at Waldoborough, who were reinforced twelve years later by a considerable addition. As, however, the title to the land was contested in the courts, a large number of them left the Muscongus and went to Orangeburg, in South Carolina. These difficulties led to an effort made by Samuel Waldo, of Falmouth (now Portland), to secure a renewal of the patent; he went to England for the purpose, and was successful. After his return to this country he went, in 1759, with Governor Pownall and a party of friends and surveyors, to his lands, ascending the Penobscot to the head of tide water. When he had reached a point where he presumed the northern line of his patent was met, he exclaimed, surveying the ground : " Here is my bound !" and dropped dead on the spot. A leaden plate, on which the sad accident was recorded, was deposited in that place, and now marks the site of the city of Bangor. The patent soon passed into the hands of the Commonwealth and there was an end to the land of Muscongus.

Another forgotten land lay almost adjoining the unfortunate Patent of Waldo. It had been granted in the earliest days of our existence by the great Council of that famous company established " at Plymouth in the county of Devon for planting, ruling and governing of New England in North America " (November, 1620). Men had flocked there already in crowds, years before, and the greatest among them had naïvely confessed the purpose of all their exertions. Captain John Smith, to whom New England owes its name, writes : " In the moneth of April, 1614, with two ships from London, I chanced to arrive in New England, a part of Ameryca, at the Isle of Monahiggan : our plot was there to take whales and make Tryalls of a Myne of Gold and Copper," (A Descr. of New Eng., 1616). Now, two members of this Great Council of Plymouth were ambitious to try a like experiment of establishing colonies on their own responsibility, and for that purpose obtained several large tracts of land. The first, granted in May, 1621, covered all the land from Maumkeag River, round Cape Ann to Merrimac River, and up these rivers to the farthest head; this district they called Mariana; but as no successful effort was made to settle it, the name soon disappeared from maps and charts, and was speedily forgotten. It was very different, however, with the grant which contemplated the erection of a province that should extend from Western Vermont through Upper Canada, over all the great lakes, and which, on this account, obtained in August, 1622, the name of Laconia. These regions were long thought to be rich in metals, diamonds and precious stones, but here as everywhere else the bright glitter of gold was only used to allure the credulous and covetous, while men of sense engaged in this enterprise for the same simple but sound reason, which was the prime motive of many of the greatest ventures of that day. They knew the abundance of fish that could be obtained from ocean and lake alike, and in those days of frequent fasts and an enormous consumption of salted provisions, fish was an article of great importance, and sure to bring enormous profits. Hence, the ambition to earn great fame as a discoverer of new regions, the hope of ruling as absolute master over princely domains, and the eager desire to render signal services to a great sovereign—these had all, no doubt, been powerful motives with the early navigators. But a more powerful inducement even, was the large profit to be made by engaging in fisheries on new and untried ground. Ever since Cabot's voyage had made known to the world the almost marvellous abundance of fish on the north-eastern shores of our Continent, these fishing-grounds have proved an irresistible attraction to high and low. Before Columbus set foot upon the Western Continent, bold fishermen had been in our waters; and the very first charter which passed under the Great Seal of England for the establishment of a colony in Newfoundland under Sir Henry Gilbert, mentions this purpose expressly. The same motive brought Sir George Calvert, the Catholic, to his colony of Avalon, and induced the Lord Chief Justice of England with others, thirteen years before the Pilgrim Fathers came to Plymouth, to turn their eyes towards New England. Even with the latter the question of fisheries was of great importance, and now it assumed once more its most attractive form, in alluring two shrewd members of the great Plymouth Company. One, Captain John Mason, a merchant and "sea-officer," had learned to value the advantage of such traffic while he was governor of a so-called "plantation" in Newfoundland; he was now governor of New Portsmouth in New Hampshire, and became, as his neighbors and competitors continually called him, the "bugbear" of that State. The other was Sir Ferdinando Gorges of Ashton Phillips in the County of Somerset, but now not unfrequently styled the "Palatine of Maine." With all their influence, and with all their shrewdness, these two men found it, however, a difficult task to comply with the conditions of the patent, which required a prompt planting and settling of certain parts of the district. They had little help to hope for from their neighbors, with whom they differed in faith and policy. The two proprietors were poor, and in search of manors and provinces; the other settlers had left their native land and tilled the soil of the New World, holding their lives in their hands, in order to secure equality of civil rights and religious privileges. Mason and Gorges were ardent monarchists and zealous Episcopalians; their neighbors were almost uniformly republicans and Nonconformists. Neither Mariana nor Laconia ever prospered, therefore, and when the indefatigable Sir Ferdinando, after surrendering his great New England patent, obtained in 1635 a new grant, and named the province New Somerset, he could indeed send out his nephew William Gorges to claim the lands, and hold a general court at Saco—but there the matter ended. The fact is, both men were plundered by their servants, cheated by their agents, and deserted by their tenants (I. Sullivan, Maine, p. 141). In vain had Laconia been divided and re-established as Maine, so called in honor of Henrietta Maria, the daughter of Henry IV., and wife of Charles I., because she held in her own right and as her private estate the province of "Meyne" in France, and as New Hampshire, a name derived from Hampshire in England, where Mason lived. After the death of the latter (Nov. 26, 1635,) his widow tried in like manner in vain to manage the magnificent domain. The costs exceeded, year after year, the revenues; her servants and tenants, ordered to provide for their own welfare, divided the property out among themselves in payment of arrears, and thus in a few years the superb estate was completely ruined. (Bancroft I. p. 328.) That the end was hastened by absurd efforts to establish a semblance of aristocracy in the province—"funny feudalities" they were called—need hardly be added. In 1679 New Hampshire was formally severed from Massachusetts by Charles II., and although Mason's heirs long persisted in urging their claims, Laconia was soon, and has ever since remained, a lost land.

The name of Lygonia is so much like that of Gorges and Mason's province, and has so long remained without any key to its original meaning, that many authors have supposed the two to be but modified forms of the same name. This suggestion appeared to be all the more forcible as the lands of Laconia, and those of Lygonia were frequently misrepresented as identical. But a somewhat more careful examination shows clearly that the resemblance of the two names is purely accidental. (I. Sullivan, Maine, p. 268.) Lygonia was a district covering not less than forty square miles, and stretching from Harpswell to the Kennebeck, which was in 1630 set aside for the first colony of farmers. The land proved, however, unfit for such purposes; soil and seasons were alike unpropitious, and the musket and hook and line alone profitable. Nothing was done, therefore, towards settling it, and in April, 1643, the Council of Plymouth transferred the grant to Alexander Rigby, then known as a Counsellor-at-Law and a republican member of the Long Parliament, but afterwards appearing as Sir Alexander Rigby, the owner of the "Plough Patent of the Sagadahock." It conferred upon him, with the title to the land, all the powers of colonial government and the jurisdiction over the people dwelling on the banks of Saco River. He never exercised these rights in person, but, as "President and Proprietor of the Province of Lygonia," he sent over agents to claim his lands, receive his rents and hold his courts. The people refused to acknowledge his right, and the claim was virtually abandoned; much land, however, is to this day held in Maine by the numerous posterity of "Parson Jordan" through this owner of a province, and although Lygonia is a forgotten land, the legal effects of its early charter have never ceased to be felt in New England.

At nearly the same time when these fruitless efforts were made in the North to establish provinces and create baronies, a name obtained in the far South a short-lived celebrity, which is now almost entirely forgotten. It appears that, in 1630, Charles I., with his usual liberality in disposing of the property of others, bestowed upon his faithful Attorney-General, Sir Robert Heath, all the lands lying in America between the 31st and 36th degree, Northern Latitude—from sea to sea! A glance at the map will show that perhaps on the whole earth no more magnificent domain could be found than the belt of States that is now contained in this truly royal gift. It was called, in honor of the king who bestowed it, Carolana; but no settlement was ever attempted, and no claim even established, for many generations. Then, all of a sudden, a somewhat remarkable personage, who has played a very prominent part in our history, Dr. Daniel Coxe, appeared, and without much difficulty obtained (in 1699) the opinion of the Attorney-General of England, that he was the true owner of the province of Carolana. Upon the strength of this official endorsement, and aided by his position as one of the proprietaries of New Jersey, the ambitious Doctor actually fitted out two exploring vessels to sound the waters of the Mississippi, and to make such discoveries as might be to his interest as owner of the vast inland territory. It was one of these ships, commanded by Barr, which met at the English Turn de Bienville, the French commander, September 10, 1699, and was by him ordered to return and never to reappear in the waters belonging to France. The precise limits of his province seem at no time to have been well known, for while, in 1650, E(dward) W(illiams), gent, published, in London, a work under the title of "Virginia, more especially the Southern part thereof Richly Truly Valued viz., the fertile Carolana and not less excellent Isle of Roanoke," Dr. Coxe himself entitled his book far more pretentiously: "A Description of the English Province of Carolana, by the Spaniards called Florida, and by the French called Louisiana, London, 1722."

It is difficult to understand how the empty sound could have maintained itself so many years in print and public use, after the substance had long since disappeared and new names had been substituted for the old designation. For in the meantime great and permanent changes had taken place in what might once have been Carolana. A brave mariner from the famous seaport of Dieppe, Jean Ribault, had, in 1562, come out with two ships, full of French Huguenots, and landing on the first day of the bonny month of May near a fair and large river, had called it the River May. Then, building a fort to protect himself against his formidable neighbors, the Spaniards in Florida, he had called it in honor of his King, Charles IX., "La Caroline." Thus the new name appeared for the first time in the annals of our history, in connection with an island in the noble bay of Port Royal. (De Thon. XI. and IV., p. 531, ed. 1626.) He was followed, a year later, by René Laudonnière, another zealous Protestant, sent out by Admiral Coligny, who, landing in June, 1564, on the River May, called on the maps of those days the river Governador, had built there a new "Caroline" (Hakluyt III. 392), which became the scene of one of the most fearful massacres ever enacted on American soil. Six hundred Christian soldiers were there murdered in cold blood by Christian soldiers of another nation, "not because they were Frenchmen, but because they were heretics," as the fanatic Spaniards took care to inscribe over the exposed remains of their victims. Although the Spaniards called the bloody place San Mates, from St. Mathew's Day, on which the deed was done, the early name of Carolina was, ever after, retained in that locality, as well as in the charters and public documents of Charles I., and Cromwell (Oldmixon Hist. I, p. 458), and its use was renewed under Charles

LOST LANDS. 253

II. Already, in 1666, we are told, the "province was so called in honor of His Sacred Majesty that now is, Charles II. whom God preserve"—(A Brief Description of Carolina, in Carroll's Hist., Cole II. p. 10), and when, in 1727, the crown of Great Britain purchased both title and interest of the proprietaries of the province, and divided it into two provinces, nothing was more natural than to name them, without going back to the original name of Carolana, North and South Carolina.

The Lost Lands of our Republic are, however, by no means confined exclusively to the earliest days of our colonial existence; we have, at least, the name of one such forgotten land, which belongs to the period of our national history. In the year 1827 a map of the United States of America was published in London, on which a State was entered under the name of Franklin. This created, at first, no little wonder, as no such country had ever been known to exist, in spite of the great reverence felt for that great man. It appeared that the name was placed where Tennessee ought to have been, and thus it became evident that Franklin had been absurdly substituted for Frankland. A glance at the early history of that State helped to explain the apparent riddle. When North Carolina ceded, by an Act of Assembly, her Western territory to the United States, about 1784, the Government, for various reasons, declined to accept the offer, and the law was repealed. The good people of its rejected district then met in convention, and declared their territory to be an independent State under the name of Frankland, chosing Colonel John Sevier as their first governor. The young State was, however, but short-lived, for the scruples of Congress were speedily overcome, and in the year 1787 the Legislature met for the last time; the State came to an end by simple want of vitality (Flint II. p. 31), and the name of Frankland is almost forgotten.

THE END.

www.ingramcontent.com/pod-product-compliance
Lightning Source LLC
Chambersburg PA
CBHW021354230426
43666CB00006B/526